100 BEST IDEAS FOR Primary Math

Written by
Holly Sar Dye, M.A.

Illustrated by Becky J. Radtke

Teaching & Learning Company
1204 Buchanan St., P.O. Box 10
Carthage, IL 62321

This book belongs to

_____

Dedicated to Philip and Alec

This book was developed for the Teaching & Learning Company
by The Good Neighbor Press, Inc., Grand Junction, CO.

Cover illustration by Nancee McClure

Copyright © 1994, Teaching & Learning Company

ISBN No. 1-57310-003-X

Printing No. 9876

Teaching & Learning Company
1204 Buchanan St., P.O. Box 10
Carthage, IL 62321

TLC10003 Copyright © Teaching & Learning Company, Carthage, IL 62321

Table of Contents

Dear Teacher,

All teachers of early childhood education face real challenges in developing a quality math-based curriculum. Math is not limited to basic operations such as addition or subtraction. It is not a series of worksheets or never-ending drills. Mathematics is experiential.

Young children can learn and indeed learn best through hands-on experiences. Sorting different kinds of nuts based on their size, weight or color will always be remembered more vividly than a worksheet which may present a similar exercise. Creating opportunities with manipulatives encourages children to solve problems which might otherwise be difficult to simply visualize. Hands-on experiences capitalize on the notion that children learn through a variety of modes: visual, auditory and kinesthetic.

As teachers, we need to guide students, through a variety of exciting and meaningful hands-on experiences. Involving children in graphing of boys and girls in a classroom and creating a block center are two ways teachers can integrate math with other curriculum areas. This book provides a wealth of hands-on experiences for young children.

The *100 Best Ideas for Primary Math* presents a collection of developmentally appropriate activities for the young child. Many of the materials suggested in this book can be easily obtained or made by the teacher or parent volunteer. The appendix offers a list of companies through which you can purchase manufactured manipulatives and resources for your mathematics program.

Many activities which appear throughout this book can be adapted to meet the diverse needs of your students. Each page identifies the math skill for which the activity has been designed. The categories of math skills are arranged in order from simple to complex. This allows you to build on a solid foundation which is developmentally sound.

One-to-One Correspondence is a skill in which objects from one set can be matched to objects of another set. These activities can include the matching of shoes to socks or numerals with sets of objects.

Numbers and Counting involves an understanding of quantities. Counting can include rote counting ("1, 2, 3, 4, 5 …") and rational counting (literally counting individual objects). Counting rhymes, the number of crayons in a box and the number of letters in your name are activities that fall into this category.

Sets and Classifying relates to how objects are grouped, sorted and regrouped. For example, there may be a box in your classroom filled with toy dishes. This box of dishes represents a set. By separating the dishes into subgroups, such as cups, saucers and plates, you are classifying them.

Comparing is a task in which there is a relationship between two objects or sets. This skill is also fundamental to ordering. Distinguishing a large block from a small block involves the use of comparison.

Shapes include these geometric figures: circle, ellipse (also called oval), square, rectangle, rhombus and triangle. There are lots of fun activities which build on the basic knowledge and use of shapes, such as shape bingo, finding shapes in the environment and creating pictures based upon shapes.

Parts and Wholes is an introduction to fractions. Understanding that parts together create wholes, and wholes can be divided into parts is the precursor to more advanced work with fractions. Putting together the pieces of a puzzle or cutting an apple into four pieces are commonplace activities which fall into this category.

Ordering (also called seriation) involves the comparison of three or more objects or sets of objects. The arrangement of these objects, such as from largest to smallest is Patterning. Patterns also involve repeated sequencing. An example of patterning is red, blue, green; red, blue, green . . . .

Measurement is a system by which things are compared in the same units. Volume, weight, length, width, area and temperature are aspects of measurement. Discovering that a table is 30 plastic links long or the bowl holds 10 cups of water are activities that utilize nonstandard and standard units of measure.

Time and Money are also units of measure. Their application in daily life necessitates a special section in this book! Money is a medium of exchange. Time involves the sequencing of events and how long they last. A daily class schedule represents the idea of sequencing and duration.

Whole Number Operations include addition, subtraction, multiplication and division. This category also involves the comparison of whole numbers such as greater than, less than and equal. Five apples and three apples equals eight apples. "I have a red balloon. You have a blue balloon. We have two balloons." Whole number operations involve the use of sets. Students can add or subtract something from a set. Multiplication deals with equal quantities and their repetition. Division involves the regrouping of a large set into smaller subsets.

Fractions are an extension of parts and wholes. The terms *halves, thirds* and *fourths* can be attached to concrete pieces of a whole. An example might be two friends sharing an orange. One-half is yours; one-half is mine. Equal parts is an important concept in working with fractions.

Place Value is the concept which addresses the placement of numbers in relationship to their value. Ones, tens and hundreds are the basic place values addressed in the primary grades. A six in the tens place (6 tens) represents 60. A six in the hundreds place (6 hundreds) represents 600.

This book was organized with the classroom teacher in mind. Followed by the skills heading and activity title, one or more student outcomes are listed. These outcomes describe what the student will accomplish through his or her active involvement. A list of suggested materials is found on every activity page. In addition to the **Group Activity**, helpful suggestions can be found in **Teacher Prep**, **Opening Activity** and **One Step Further**. The sidebar on each page provides more suggestions and activities such as **Links to Science, Language Arts, Social Studies** and **Art**. **Links to Literature** highlights quality children's literature that compliments many of the activities.

Feel free to modify the activities to fit the needs of your students. If you teach using a monthly or seasonal approach, the ladybugs used in "Ladybug Match" can be changed to fall leaves and called "Fall Leaf Match." Most of all, have fun with math. Self-discovery is the greatest teacher of all!

Sincerely,

Holly

Holly Sar Dye, M.A.

1. Pass the Box

What's in the box? You're sure to intrigue students with this suspenseful matching game.

Outcome
Students will match similar objects.

Materials
- cardboard box (large enough to hold 24+ objects comfortably)
- 12 pairs of objects
- self-adhesive shelf paper

Teacher Prep
Close the box and seal the ends with adhesive tape. Carefully cut a hole in one side of the box. This hole should be large enough to accommodate the teacher's hand and the size of the objects. Using self-adhesive shelf paper, wrap the box for decoration.

Twelve pairs of items (or more depending upon the number of students) should be placed in the box. Some examples of items include die-cast cars, crayons, small blocks, paintbrushes, small stuffed animals, toy dishes, books, craft sticks, keys, musical instruments and mittens. Shake the box well to mix up the items.

Group Activity
With students assembled in a circle, demonstrate how to pull an object from the box. This should be done without looking. Students will try to match their object with the same (or similar) object another student has.

The box is passed around the circle until everyone has an object. Once objects have been selected, they should be displayed on the floor in front of the students. Going counterclockwise, each student tries to match objects with another student. The pairs of students stand together until everyone is standing with their partner.

Link to Language
After students have been paired, go around the circle again and ask each student to:

1. *Name the object they selected.*

2. *Describe what the object looks like and how it feels.*

3. *Explain how the object works or what it does.*

2. Animal Babies and Their Mothers

A popular topic for science and social studies also makes its way into your math curriculum!

Outcome
Students will identify animal babies with their mothers. Students will use one-to-one correspondence skills to make association.

Materials
- magazine pictures of animal babies and their mothers
- construction paper (to mount pictures)
- picture books about animal babies
- lamination (optional)

Teacher Prep
Create an animal picture file by selecting magazine pictures of animal babies and their mothers. Natural history and nature magazines are good sources for these kinds of pictures. Enlist the help of parent volunteers to assist in your search for animal pictures. Cut them out, mount them on colorful construction paper and laminate. Divide a classroom bulletin board into two areas labeled "Animal Babies" and "Mothers."

Group Activity
Ask one student to select a picture. If able, the student should identify what kind of animal was selected and whether it's a baby or a mother. Pin the picture to the bulletin board under the corresponding heading. Ask another student to select the corresponding picture to display on the other half of the bulletin board, directly across from the previously identified picture.

Link to Social Studies

Take a trip to the local zoo! Don't forget to stop by the petting zoo where children can get a first-hand look at animal babies. Be sure to photograph students with the animals. Set up a display area in your classroom with the photographs, plastic animal replicas and some favorite children's books on animals.

3. A Step Ahead

Challenge students to find *their* shoes while reinforcing math concepts!

Outcome
Students will make one-to-one association using shoes.

Materials
• students' shoes

Teacher Prep
None.

Group Activity
Ask students to remove their shoes. Collect shoes from students. Place pairs of shoes randomly in a line on the floor. Students should be facing away from shoes as the teacher lines up the shoes. At the signal, students should turn around and locate their own shoes. Depending upon the ability of the group, students can simply retrieve the shoes and be seated or retrieve them and put them on.

One Step Further
Mix up the shoes that are in the line to increase the challenge. Reward students with stickers when the "mixed up shoes" have been recovered.

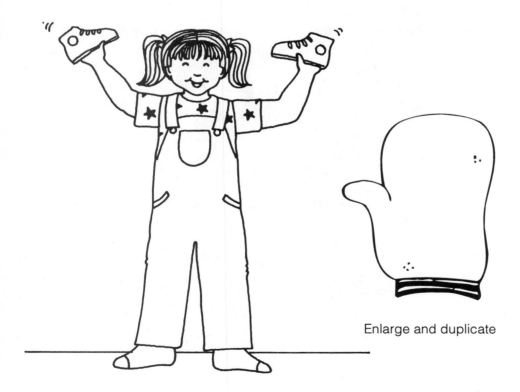

Enlarge and duplicate

Link to Literature
The Mitten, *adapted and illustrated by Jan Brett (Scholastic: New York, 1989) is a Ukrainian folktale about a boy who lost one of his mittens. Several animals squeeze together in the mitten to make a home. Using the mitten pattern on this page, duplicate several pairs of mittens in a variety of colors. Laminate them for durability and cut around the bold lines. Store the paper mittens in a small basket or an envelope. After reading the story to your class, leave the book out with the mitten match game. Students can play in a small group, pairs or individually trying to match all the paper mittens. For a greater challenge, duplicate the mitten pattern on varying shades of several colors. For example, one pair of mittens could be light green, another a pair dark green and another pair yellow-green.*

4. Coming to Lunch?

Give your eager students an opportunity to lend a helping hand at mealtime and practice correspondence skills.

Outcomes
Students will set a number of places at a table to correspond with the number of students in the classroom. Students will exercise "life skills" at school.

Materials
- plates, napkins, cups and eating utensils for each student in class
- table and chairs to accommodate all students

To the Teacher
Life skills are those tasks which everyone needs to learn in order to function. Examples include getting dressed, hygiene, nutrition and social interaction. Students should be encouraged to participate in these tasks as often as possible. Have different students help to set up morning and afternoon snack, preparing cots or mats for nap time, assisting in the setup and serving of lunch. Remember, adults and children like to feel a sense of community spirit and accomplishment that can be experienced outside of an academic or traditional curriculum.

Teacher Prep
Little preparation is needed for this activity! Items that you might normally use for snack time or lunch should be readily available. Different students can be asked to assist with setup. It's up to you. Perhaps you would like three or four students to set the table at lunch time and a different set of students to set the table at snack time.

Link to Social Studies
Take advantage of mealtime as a time to learn about other cultures. Occasionally prepare a snack, dessert or main dish from another country or culture. Involve students in the preparation of the dish. Play music from the same country as everyone feasts. Decide how often you want to participate in the cooking project. Perhaps some parents would volunteer to bring a dish from their country of origin or help teach the students how to prepare a dish!

5. What's in the Bag?

Imagine the curiosity and excitement of your students when you enter the classroom with twenty paper bags, filled with . . .

Outcome
Students will correspond a number with a given set of objects.

Materials
• 20 lunch-sized paper bags
• 20 index cards numbered 1-20
• 20 clothespins
• 20 different kinds of objects: in quantities increasing from 1 to 20

Teacher Prep
The teacher should prepare each bag before initiating the activity. Each bag will contain different objects and will differ in quantity. For example: the first bag may contain one die-cast car, the second bag may contain two crayons, the third bag may contain three blocks and so on.

Opening Activity
Place the number cards in a pocket chart, on a chalkboard tray or any similar display area. Randomly select a number card and ask a student to find that number of objects within the classroom. Suggested items that are easily accessible may include books, puzzle pieces, plastic dishes or pieces of construction paper. Give each student an opportunity to make the one-to-one correspondence.

Group Activity
Allow students to work in small groups as they are randomly given paper bags the teacher has previously filled. Display the twenty number cards so they can be accessed by students. Students then count the objects in one bag, find the corresponding number card and attach it to the paper bag with a clothespin. Encourage students to continue in this fashion until all bags have been labeled.

One Step Further
Increase the difficulty of this activity by mixing the objects from the various bags. In this way the students will be less likely to associate a number with a particular object. For more advanced students, use only one kind of object, such as die-cast cars. This will depend upon your ability to obtain 210 of the same object.

Link to Language
If you are doing a thematic unit, locate or create objects for the paper bags which will correspond with your theme. If you are studying the ocean and shells aren't readily available, design your own on paper, duplicate and laminate. Clip art is also a great resource in a pinch!

6. Personal Puzzles

Learning your name was never so much fun!

Outcome

Students will use one-to-one correspondence while identifying the letters of their first names.

Materials

- 3" or 4" letter stencils or traceable letters
- 2 sheets of construction paper per student
- pencil
- scissors
- sandwich bag to store letters

Teacher Prep

Using uppercase letter stencils, outline the first name of each student on the first sheet of construction paper. Outline the name again on the second sheet of construction paper. Cut out the letters made on the second sheet of construction paper. Mix up the letters and store them in a sandwich bag, labeled with the student's name.

Group Activity

Before the activity is started, the teacher should print the first name of each student on a large index card. During morning circle time, the teacher shows one name card at a time. Students are instructed to approach the teacher and take the card if the card spells their first name. This is a good review activity that can be played regularly.

When all students have had their turn, they may return to their seats. Distribute the first piece of construction paper which has the name of the student outlined. Give each student the corresponding bag of letters. Instruct students to match each of the letters in the bag to the construction paper "mat." Students who are able to complete the activity successfully can receive a sticker or some other type of incentive.

One Step Further

Once students have mastered this activity, increase the difficulty by creating last name puzzles, number puzzles or shape puzzles. This is also a good activity for teaching children their telephone numbers. Extend the activity for teaching children their telephone numbers. Extend the activity by involving parents! Send home the "mat" and corresponding pieces with a brief set of directions.

Link to Science

Enlist the help of students in mixing the ingredients of a favorite cookie recipe. Sugar, peanut butter or gingerbread allow for a smooth consistency. Using letter cookie cutters, ask each student to select the cutter which represents the first letter in his or her name. Then direct the student to cut a cookie from the mixture. Bake according to the directions. Allow students to decorate their cookies with icing and multicolored sprinkles! Enjoy!

Ladybug Match

Outcome
Students will become familiar with numerals and the quantities they represent.

Materials
- file folder
- several copies of ladybug pattern
- black, self-adhesive dots
- glue
- scissors
- marking pen
- lamination (optional)

Teacher Prep
Enlarge and duplicate twenty ladybug patterns on red paper. Trim the copies and select ten to be mounted on the inside of the file folder (five on each side). Randomly affix black, self-adhesive dots on the ladybugs. There should be one dot on one bug, two dots on the next, three on the next and so on until the final ladybug has ten dots.

Affix black dots on the remaining ladybug patterns in the same way: one dot on the first ladybug, two dots on the next, three on the next until you have placed ten dots on the tenth ladybug. (Optional: Laminate the folder and number cards for durability.)

Group Activity
Students match each spotted ladybug card with a ladybug on the folder containing the same amount of spots. This can be done individually, in pairs or in small groups. Students check answers with a buddy or the teacher. **Rational counting** (assigning a number to an object—see "Numbers and Counting" in the introduction) is also strengthened through this activity.

One Step Further
- There are lots of variations to this game. By replacing the spots on the ladybug cards with numbers, you have created another **rational counting** activity. This self-checking version can include small black dots made on the backs of the number cards to correspond with each number.

- For additional readiness practice, change the dots on the gameboard to number words! Older students can utilize the gameboard for a self-checking addition/subtraction game: Write facts on the gameboard ladybugs, answers on the remaining pattern cards with dots on the back to correspond with the answers.

Enlarge and duplicate

Links to Science and Literature
Observe the wonders of ladybugs! These fascinating creatures are available seasonally at many nurseries or garden shops. Ladybugs help in pest control by eating aphids, commonly found on flowers and plants.

For a final activity, read and discuss **The Grouchy Ladybug** *by Eric Carle. HarperTrophy (A Division of HarperCollins Publishers), 1986. This story chronicles the grouchy ladybug's encounters with various members of the animal kingdom. Small clock faces and hands are featured on most pages where the ladybug meets a new animal. A great book for teaching time, sequence of events and size comparison.*

8. Pegging Numbers

Make the connection between abstract and concrete with a little help from a pegboard and some pegs!

Outcome
Students will associate numbers with concrete objects.

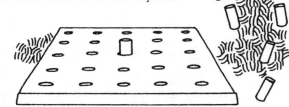

Materials
- 25-hole pegboard
- 25 or more pegs
- number cards 1-20
- felt-tip marker

To the Teacher
The pegboard is a wonderful classroom tool. It has many applications in the areas of mathematics and readiness. The materials from which pegboards and pegs are made vary: sponge-like material, plastic and wood are the most common. Allow your students to experiment with this manipulative. Some pegs are made to stack one on top of the other for an added dimension in mathematics.

Teacher Prep
Preparation for this experience is minimal. Obtain one or more pegboards and one or more sets of pegs. Number cards can be purchased or made simply from index cards. For the purpose of self-checking, draw lines on the back of each number card to indicate the number of pegs which would be represented by the number on the front.

Group Activity
Put two or three pegs of different colors on the pegboard. Ask students to find a matching peg (from the extras laying on the table or floor) and put it next to a peg of the same color on the board.

For a more challenging activity, show students a number card and ask one volunteer to put the same number of pegs in the pegboard. Continue the activity until every child has had one or several turns.

Students can also find patterns among the pegs on the board. Try creating a pattern, but leave out one or two pegs. Ask students if they know which is the missing peg!

By obtaining several pegboards the opportunities for individual student participation are increased.

Link to Readiness
Randomly place various colored pegs on the board. Have students name the color of the peg as you touch it. The teacher should move her finger left to right, top to bottom. In this way, reading readiness skills are reinforced!

9. Bottles and Tops

Don't discard those empty, plastic bottles . . . recycle them in these unlimited ways.

Outcome
Students will be able to match bottles with their corresponding tops.

Materials

- several different sizes and shapes of plastic bottles; one- or two-liter soda bottles, dish soap bottles, hand soap bottles/dispensers, plastic baby bottles, plastic salad dressing bottles, etc.
- 2 cardboard boxes

Teacher Prep
Other than obtaining bottles, clean them out thoroughly. You may wish to leave the label intact. Avoid using bottles that contained any poisonous substance or drug.

Separate the bottles from their tops and place them in separate boxes or containers.

Group Activity
Students take turns selecting a bottle, then matching top. If the match is incorrect, the pieces go back in their respective boxes, and another student takes a turn.

The game can be made more difficult by students closing their eyes as they select the objects. Another variation: Each student selects one bottle or one top. Students then try to find their matching part which another student has.

One Step Further
Bottles and tops make a versatile manipulative! Students can find objects which would fit into the caps (one-to-one correspondence). They can also be used for *patterning*. Graph the kinds of bottles you have with your students. Possible chart headings could be beverages, cleaning agents and food.

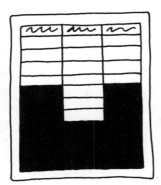

Link to Art
Transform your empty plastic bottle into a puppet's head! Add wiggly eyes, yarn hair (or a mop head for larger bottles), a nose and mouth made from construction paper. Insert a wooden dowel through the bottle's opening. Glue a piece of cloth remnant around the neck of the bottle for "clothing." Students will have lots of fun playing with the new class puppet! Display it proudly in your dramatic play area.

10. Number Museum

Introduce students to the world of numbers by creating a mini math museum right in your own classroom.

Outcome

Students will be familiar with the importance of numbers in our daily lives. They will experiment with items such as the abacus, calculator and number line.

Materials

- abacus
- hand-held calculator
- adding machine with tape
- number line 1-100
- slide rule
- toy cash register
- play money and sorting tray
- toy telephone
- food packaging (empty and clean)
- measuring spoons and cups
- ruler and tape measure
- patterns for making clothes (available in most sewing shops)
- clocks: analog with and without Roman numerals, digital clock, wristwatch, hourglass, kitchen timer, etc.
- display table and tablecloth

Teacher Prep

Prepare a large table by covering it with a colorful table-cloth. The table should be at a height which is accessible to all students. Randomly set the math-related objects on the table.

Group Activity

Assemble students in a semicircle on the floor or carpet. Ask students where they see numbers in their home, school and community. Give an example by sharing a toy telephone. Demonstrate where the numbers are and how they are used. Call on students to select an item from the number museum and share it with the class. Encourage students to explain how the numbers are important to us. Send a note home during the week asking parents to send in items from home that have some sort of reference to math: postage stamps, foreign currency, clothing labels which indicate size, various sized mixing bowls, a remote control device, a portable radio, etc. Remind parents to label items with their names so they can be returned. Add items to your display table and discuss them daily.

Link to Language

Take photographs of students with museum objects. Record student explanations of how the objects are used and their math importance on an audiotape. Display photos and play the audiotape at Open House or Back-to-School night.

11. Celebrate 100

Create your own classroom holiday by counting the first one hundred days of school!

Outcome
Students will become familiar with the numbers 1 through 100.

Materials
- various collections of objects which contain 100 items
- pocket "hundreds" chart (available commercially) or
- poster board and marking pen
- stickers for "hundreds" chart
- party decorations
- ingredients for baking a cake

To the Teacher
Young children delight in celebrating special occasions. For some teachers, circle time provides the opportunity to discuss the day's weather, what month of the year and day of the week it is. An additional function of the calendar is to assist in documenting the first one hundred days of school. By placing the numbers on the chart in order from left to right, top to bottom, you also facilitate reading readiness skills.

Teacher Prep
Obtain a pocket chart for use with numbers 1-100 or using a piece of poster board, create a grid of one hundred blank squares. Entitle your chart "Celebrate 100 Days of School."

Opening Activity
Introduce the idea of one hundred by bringing a collection of one hundred objects to class. Perhaps one hundred children's books, one hundred crayons, one hundred buttons, one hundred blocks and so on. Every week or two, introduce a new 100 collection as a center activity.

Group Activity
As you discuss the calendar each day with your class, document the number of days students have been in school by selecting a child to place a sticker on the 100 chart.

On the final week of the count, prepare for your 100th Day Party. Teachers and students can decorate the room with a banner, streamers and balloons. Decorate a special bulletin board in your classroom with a three-layer paper cake and one hundred candles. Students can include their families by making party invitations and inviting them to the classroom celebration.

Links to Math and Science
Allow students to help you prepare a real cake for the class party. Math and science skills reinforced by this activity include counting and measuring ingredients and observing thermal reaction. Have students observe the cake several times throughout the baking process. Ask such questions as: What changes do you see in the cake? (The cake is rising.) What is causing the cake to change? (Heat causes the cake to change.)

On the 100th day, celebrate the culmination of activities and preparation by marking the 100th day on the class chart with a special sticker and serving cake (see Links to Math and Science on previous page).

Activity Center

Set up an activity center with varying sizes of Styrofoam™ circles for cake layers, bakers' tools, a chef's hat and apron, party plates and candles. Make a stove out of a cardboard box.

12. Number Collage

Create meaning for numbers and learn about sets in this very hands-on project.

Outcome
Students will locate pictures of objects which represent specific numbers.

Materials
- several magazines
- poster board
- colored markers
- scissors
- paste or glue

Teacher Prep
None required other than obtaining materials.

Group Activity
Divide class into small table groups. Each group gets a piece of poster board with a large numeral written in the center. Instruct students to find sets of objects in the magazines which represent the number written in the middle. Cut them out and paste them to the poster board.

For example, students may find a cooking picture that has three cookies in it to match their number three on the poster. Another group of students can't find a set of ten cars to match their number ten, so they create their own set of ten cars from an assortment of single pictures.

Display the finished posters around the room. When studying numbers or sets, it may be helpful to make reference to the student-made posters.

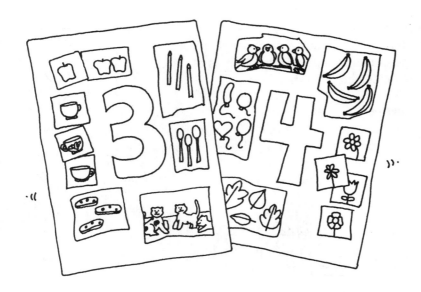

Link to Literature
What Comes in 2's, 3's, & 4's? *by Suzanne Aker (Simon & Schuster Inc.: New York, 1990). This counting book introduces the numbers 2, 3 and 4 to young children by presenting objects found in daily life. It is a fabulous picture book for preschoolers. Use it as an introduction to sets, then advance to the poster project.*

13. Feely Flash Cards

These tactile flash cards are sure to be a hit in any classroom!

Outcome
Students will become familiar with numbers through the sense of touch.

Materials
- large index cards
- glue
- scissors
- sandpaper
- buttons
- pom-poms
- felt
- dried beans
- heavy string
- velvet
- craft fur
- silk
- coins
- large number stencils (optional)

Teacher Prep
Decide which medium you will use for each number (for example: craft fur shaped as a number 1). Those appearing in the materials list are *only* suggestions! Cut out or lay out large numbers from each of the different media. Glue one number to each of the index cards (in some cases, hot glue may be most effective). **Note:** Index cards should be used vertically. If you are not comfortable creating a block number free-hand, use large number stencils or a template as a guide.

Group Activity
Students can be asked to select and identify a card. They can also create sets of objects, such as blocks, to represent the selected number card.

One Step Further
Treat individual students to a set of their own feely flash cards! Accompanied by a note suggesting one or two ways in which the cards can be used, the cards also facilitate parent involvement at home.

Link to Art
Save your scraps from the "Feely Flash Cards" project and have students make textured collages. Lightweight cardboard, a large index card or a piece of construction paper can be used as a surface on which students can glue or paste scraps.

14. Red Bean Numbers

Students will become engrossed as they make their own manipulative flash cards!

Outcome
Students will make tactile numbers using red beans.

Materials
- bag of uncooked, red beans
- 5" x 8" (12.7 x 20.32 cm) blank index cards
- white glue
- pencil

Teacher Prep
Determine the numbers you want students to practice. For young children, 1-10 may be sufficient. Older students can make cards representing the numbers 1-20. The cards do not have to be made all on the same day. If you are presenting a number each week, make cards only for those numbers in that particular week. Store them in resealable, plastic freezer bags. Save the cards until you have completed your "deck." Send them home with a note which explains what the child did in class.

Group Activity
This is a great "beginner's" activity. Lightly in pencil, the teacher (or student if he or she is able) writes one number on each card. Numbers should not be small, but not too large. Trace over the line with white glue. Students put red beans on the white glue, completely covering the "trail." Beans should be touching each other – no spaces between beans and no overlapping. Set the cards aside to dry.

One Step Further
There are endless possibilities for extended activities! Create a second set of red bean cards, identical to the first set. Rubber stamp groups of objects on separate index cards to match the red bean number cards. Use them for One-to-One Correspondence activities. Use red beans and glue to outline basic shapes. For older children, red beans can be used as counters for Whole Number Operations.

Link to Literature
Mouse Count by Ellen Stoll Walsh (Harcourt Brace Jovanovich, 1991) is about a snake who finds, counts and collects ten mice that he plans to eat for dinner. The mice, however, outsmart the snake in the end! Students can help count the mice and "uncount" the mice as the teacher shares this book aloud with students.

15. Clap, Stomp, Shout

Learning about numbers can be lots of fun when you use your whole body!

Outcome
Students will demonstrate tasks a designated number of times.

Materials
- 2 paper bags
- 2 3" x 5" (7.62 x 12.7 cm) index cards per student
- pencil
- outdoor space

Teacher Prep
Prepare two sets of index cards, one set for each paper bag. On the first set, write one number on each card. Duplication of numbers may be necessary depending on the ability of your students. The number of cards you make for both sets should be equal to the number of students playing. On the second set of cards, create a series of tasks. Again, one per card. Some suggestions include clap your hands, stomp your left foot, shout your name, hop on one foot, jump on two feet, walk around the swings, pat your head, blink your eyes, etc.

Group Activity
Students draw one card from each bag, then perform the task as many times as the number card indicates. For example, Paul draws a number 6 card and a "hop on one foot" card. Paul must then hop on one foot 6 times! If the task is not compromised, let the student count aloud while doing the task. If this isn't possible, encourage the group to do the counting.

Link to Math
Create patterns such as stomp your left foot three times, clap once, stomp your right foot three times, clap once again. Then repeat the pattern several times. As students start to understand the game and patterns, create a longer sequence or a more complicated one! You can even leave out one of the movements and let the students guess what should come next.

16. A Play on Numbers

Students assume the roles of animals in Galdone's, *Over in the Meadow.*

Outcome

Students will review concepts of sequencing and quantity and will associate numerals with quantities as they perform a nursery counting rhyme.

Materials

- *Over in the Meadow* by Paul Galdone (Simon and Schuster, 1986)
- lamination (optional)
- soft, instrumental music (optional)
- animal reproducibles (page 103)
- tongue depressors
- colored markers

Teacher Prep

Photocopy and enlarge the animal reproducibles. You need the following quantities:

1 turtle	3 beavers	5 bees	7 ducks	9 fish
2 frogs	4 mice	6 crows	8 pigs	10 foxes

After coloring the animals with markers, laminate them for durability and mount them on tongue depressors. Because there are a total of 55 animals, you may want to assign the parts in this way:

1 student — turtle	2 students — 3 crows each
2 students — frogs	2 students — 3 ducks and 4 ducks
3 students — beavers	2 students — 4 pigs each
4 students — mice	2 students — 4 fish and 5 fish
1 student — 5 bees	2 students — 5 foxes each

This is an arrangement for a class of 21 students. Adjust the parts to create fewer or more roles. It's important that every student participates!

Students that are assigned three, four or five animals can mount them on construction paper instead of tongue depressors for greater ease in handling.

Group Activity

Over in the Meadow is a charming book students will want to hear over and over! Assemble students for your story time. As you are reading the story aloud, encourage students to "respond" to mother's commands (i.e. "Quack, said the mother.").

Discuss the idea of a class play based on Galdone's book. Ask for student volunteers to fill the parts. As the teacher reads the introduction to the numbers, each animal or set of animals walks onto the stage or in front of the classroom. The animals respond in a chorus to mother's command each time:

Mother Frog (Teacher): "Jump, said the mother."
Frogs (2 students): "We jump, said the two."

Link to Art
Create a large mural of Galdone's meadow for a backdrop in your class play! Things to include are a sun, grass, sand, blue pond, upright and fallen trees, red barn with door, wildflowers, a nest, barnyard gate, stream and a den.

17. My Own Counting Book

Are you studying fall leaves, weather, apples or beans? Integrate symbols from these thematic units with numbers to create a very special counting book.

Outcome
Students will make individual counting books with numbers and representational amounts.

Materials
- 11 5" x 8" (12.70 x 20.32 cm) index cards per student
- stickers, decorative paper punch or clip art
- hole punch
- 1 loose-leaf metal ring per student
- marking pen

Teacher Prep
Create a cover for the student books using one of the eleven index cards. If you are doing a theme unit on bears, use bear stickers, clip art or decorative punches to illustrate the cover. Use a catchy title such as *A "Beary" Exciting Counting Book*. The teacher, a classroom parent or students (depending on ability) write the numeral and number word on each of the remaining ten cards.

Group Activity
Each day, have students decorate one or two cards with bears. The number of bears on each card should match the numeral on the card. When the page(s) have been completed, punch a single hole in the top left corner of each card. Secure them with a loose-leaf metal ring (available in many stationery stores).

One Step Further
The loose-leaf ring allows you to add more cards later! Don't feel you must stop at the number ten. What about numbers 11-20?

Link to Literature
*If you like the idea of using a bear theme, don't miss **Numbears: A Counting Book** by Kathleen Hague (Scholastic: New York, 1990). This counting book emphasizes the numbers 1-12. Each bear in this rhyming story does something different to correspond with each of the twelve numbers. Make bear masks out of paper plates and put on a **Numbears** play!*

18. Which Does Not Belong?

Can you find out which set is unlike the rest?

Outcome

Students will count objects and will be able to discriminate between like and unlike quantities.

Materials

- connecting cubes, colored chips or tiles, plastic links, craft sticks or any other manipulative used in counting
- a surface, such as a table or the floor
- number cards 1-20

Teacher Prep

None required other than obtaining materials.

Group Activity

This game is best done in smaller groups. Select a number and arrange counters to correspond with the number. Several sets representing that number should be placed on the table or floor. Space the sets out so students can distinguish between the groupings. Insert one set of counters that **does not** correspond with the rest of the sets. Challenge students on different levels: What number is represented by most of the groups? Which set does not belong? Why? Have students answer the questions using the number cards when it's appropriate.

Link to Art

Equip students with white construction paper and crayons, markers or paint. Tell them to select an object to draw. There is no limit as to the number of objects the students draw. Collect the drawings and group them according to the number of objects in each picture. For example: Tony draws five trees, Dwayne draws three cars and Kelly draws five balloons. Tony and Kelly's pictures will be sorted together because both pictures contain a group of five.

Use this activity to expand upon the idea of sorting and classification. Pictures can be grouped by number of objects they have in common, types of objects, color and size of objects.

19. Lots of Apples

Make lots of apples, tack one on top of the other and they'll never fall down!

Outcome
Students will perform rational counting from 1-10.

Materials
- apple pattern (at bottom of page)
- red paper for duplication
- scissors
- glue
- white construction paper on which to mount apples
- *Ten Apples Up on Top!* by Theodore Geisel (A Dr. Suess book—Random House, Inc: New York, 1961)

Teacher Prep
This activity is best done over several days. Enlarge and duplicate the apple pattern below onto red paper. The teacher or students can cut around the apple patterns.

Group Activity
Assemble the students and introduce them to the Dr. Suess book, *Ten Apples Up on Top!* Ask students what they think the book is about by looking at the front cover and hearing the title.

Read the book aloud, stopping as students wish to make comments or ask questions. With the help of student volunteers, count the number of apples or sets of apples on each page.

Introduce the activity by demonstrating what students are expected to do. Cut out one apple and glue it to one piece of construction paper. Then cut out two apples, stack them one on top of the other and glue them in place on a second sheet of construction paper. Each day, do one or two numbers represented by stacking apples.

One Step Further
Create apple word problems. Students "perform" the various number parts using their apple stacks. For example: Danny has 1 apple, Mel has 4 apples and Joy has 2 apples. How many apples do they have in all? Each student goes to the front of the room with 1, 4, and 2 apples respectively. Ask the rest of the class to solve the problem by counting Danny's, Mel's and Joy's apples!

Link to Art
Purchase several apples. Cut some apples in half vertically, and the others horizontally. Ask students what they notice about the inside of the apples after they have been cut. Using red, green and yellow poster paints and construction paper, have students make apple prints. Simply dip one half of an apple into paint, making sure the fleshy part is thoroughly covered, and press onto construction paper for an image. Select apples with both cut designs to dip and press. Allow the prints to dry and mount on colored construction paper. Display artwork around the classroom.

Enlarge and duplicate

20. What's Your Favorite Jelly Bean?

Everyone has a favorite jelly bean. Is it licorice, cherry or the light green one?

Outcome

Students will identify their favorite jelly bean. They will survey people, record data, graph preferences, compare numbers and report results in class.

Materials

- bag of jelly beans, containing a variety of colors
- butcher paper
- colored markers
- "What's Your Favorite Jelly Bean?" record sheet

Teacher Prep

Prepare a chart with the title "What's Your Favorite Jelly Bean?" Create as many columns on the chart as you need. Duplicate the record sheet for each student.

Group Activity

Assemble students in a semicircle. Show students the different colored jelly beans. Ask students to name the colors. Record their responses on the chalkboard or marker board. Select the colors you want represented on the chart and write them in. Ask students individually to name their favorite jelly bean. Record student names under the appropriate colors, or use photographs of students to indicate preferences. Determine the most popular and least popular jelly beans according to the student responses.

One Step Further

- Have students conduct a similar survey at home. Students can record responses from siblings, parents or neighborhood friends. Instruct students to return the sheet the next morning. Record the responses on the class chart and discuss the findings.

- Have students create number sentences on index cards with the jelly beans. For example: 3 green jelly beans and 1 red jelly bean equals 4 jelly beans. Older students can write the number three in green crayon with three green jelly beans underneath the number. Do the same thing with the number one, written in red and represented with one red jelly bean drawn underneath it. Don't forget the addition sign and equal sign. Write the number four as the answer with three green jelly beans and one red one underneath the four.

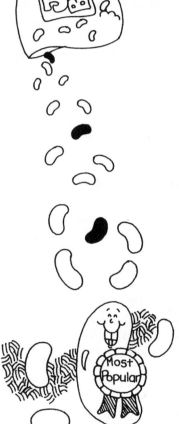

Link to Social Studies

Lead a small or large group discussion with this question, "What is your favorite thing?" Perhaps it's a special doll or stuffed animal. Maybe it's a book or carton character. After the group activity, have students draw and color their favorite thing. Display the pictures on a bulletin board with the heading "Room __'s Favorite Things."

21. Number Recognition Bingo

This bingo game will provide endless fun for students! Played in pairs, this game encourages students to help each other.

Outcome
Students will recognize numbers as they are called out.

Materials
- bingo cards
- dried bean markers
- number tiles from 1 to 20
- stickers for winners (optional)

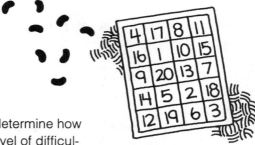

Teacher Prep
In making bingo cards, you should determine how many students will be playing and level of difficulty at which the game will be set. Several additional cards should be made beyond the number of students playing.

The teacher decides how many squares each card should have and randomly places numbers in them.

Group Activity
Students are paired off and given one card. The teams place dried beans on the numbers as they are called out. The first team to mark an entire line of numbers either vertically or horizontally is the winner.

One Step Further
- In place of calling out numbers, call out simple addition/subtraction facts. Students mark the answers on their bingo card.

- If your curriculum focuses on a special theme, try using markers or counters that fit the theme, too. Perhaps your class is studying dinosaurs. Obtain a bulk quantity of plastic dinosaurs to mark the numbers on the bingo cards.

Link to Spelling
For older children, prepare bingo cards that have number words. For example, instead of using 1, 2, 3, . . . write the words one, two, three . . . . As the teacher calls out the numbers, students look for the correctly spelled word!

22. M & M's® and Estimation

This tasty math activity has high appeal to chocolate lovers!

Outcome
Students will estimate the number of candies in a jar and check their estimation by counting the candies.

Materials
- large bag of M & M's®
- clear plastic jar
- class chart

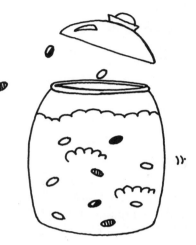

Teacher Prep
After obtaining a jar, fill it with M & M's® chocolate candies. Depending upon the size of your jar, you may need more than one large bag of candy. With younger children, it would be better to select a small jar and control the amount of M & M's® so students can feel success in counting with little or no frustration.

Group Activity
Assemble students in a circle on the floor. Before introducing them to the candy jar, have students practice counting to one hundred. This can be done by students "counting off:" 1, 2, 3, 4, 5, 6, 7, 8, 9, ... When each student has said his or her number, continue going around, maintaining the number sequence until you have reached one hundred.

After you've practiced counting, pass the M & M's® jar around the circle. Ask each student to think about how many chocolate candies are in the jar. Pass the jar around a second time, this time asking each student to judge the amount or *estimate* aloud. The teacher records the estimations on a class chart.

When everyone has had a chance to estimate the amount of candies in the jar, pour out the contents onto a piece of clean butcher paper. Students can organize the candy into piles of ten, then determine the total by counting all the tens and remaining ones. The teacher can encourage students to draw conclusions comparing the estimates with the actual data:

1. Which estimate was the closest to the actual number of M & M's®?
2. Which estimate was furthest from the actual number of M & M's®?
3. What would be another way to count the M & M's®?

One Step Further
Challenge students to create patterns using the M & M's®. Other activities include sorting the candies by color and graphing students' favorite colors.

Link to Literature
The M & M's® Brand Chocolate Candies Counting Book *by Barbara Barbieri McGrath (Charlesbridge, 1994) is a picture book containing math activities children can do with M & M's®: counting with color identification, creating and adding to sets, shapes and whole number operations. Students will have lots of fun with this book!*

23. Fractional Counters

Say good-bye to abstract fractions with this practical activity.

Outcome
Students will use fractions to describe results in an experiment.

Materials
- two-color counters (red/yellow or red/white)
- paper cup
- tally chart (see illustration)

$\dfrac{0}{4}$	$\dfrac{1}{4}$	$\dfrac{2}{4}$	$\dfrac{3}{4}$	$\dfrac{4}{4}$

Teacher Prep
No preparation required other than obtaining materials.

Group Activity
Divide the class into several small groups. Each group needs four two-color counters, a paper cup and a tally chart. Putting the counters in the cup, students then cover the top of the cup with one hand and shake vigorously. The counters should then be "dumped" onto the floor or table. What fraction represents the number of red counters faceup? The total number of counters is 4. This number becomes the *denominator* of the fraction. The number of red counters faceup is the *numerator* of the fraction. The numerator over the denominator is the *fraction*.

Students take turns shaking the counters, dumping them and identifying the fraction. For each fraction, a tally should be recorded under the appropriate column on the tally chart. Have students perform this task ten times. Ask students what they observe from their charts. Perform the task ten more times. What happens to the results?

One Step Further
Use poker chips instead of two-color counters. Put four poker chips in a paper bag: 1 white and 3 red. Shake the bag and pull out a chip. What color did you pull out? What fraction does this represent: ¼ or ¾? Are you three times more likely to pull out a red chip? Why?

Link to Science
Give each student four crackers. On one cracker, students can spread peanut butter (or another substitute). On the other three crackers, students can spread jam. One-fourth of the crackers are peanut butter versus three-fourths that are jam!

24. The Button Sort

Button, button, who's got the button? Everyone, in all kinds of shapes, colors and sizes!

Outcome

Students will sort buttons by shape, size, color or other identifying attributes.

Materials

- bag of buttons (available in one-half to one-pound bags through various arts and crafts suppliers)
- sorting trays: egg cartons, muffin tins, small tackle boxes (with several sections), etc.

To the Teacher

Attributes are characteristics. These characteristics (or features) can include size, shape, color and/or thickness. Attribute blocks (commercially made) are shapes (circles, squares, rectangles and triangles) which usually come in 3 colors, 2 sizes and 2 thicknesses. Buttons are more readily available and far less expensive. If purchasing a bag of buttons is not feasible, start collecting them from neighbors, parents or friends. A quick note in your classroom or school newsletter, "Room ____ is collecting any and all kinds of buttons. Can you help?" may yield some exciting results.

Note: The use of small buttons may not be appropriate for children who have a tendency to put objects in their mouths. Large, plastic buttons are commercially available for these children.

Teacher Prep

No preparation required other than obtaining materials.

Group Activity

This activity is more effective in small groups or individually (as in an activity center). Ask students to name the ways they can sort the buttons you have displayed. Some answers may include by color, by weight, by size and by how they feel (smooth versus textured). Suggest students select one attribute or feature by which they can sort the buttons. For example, if a student selects color, then each impression in the egg carton would represent a different color: red, blue, green, orange, yellow, black, brown, purple, white, silver, gold and mixed. Many hours can be spent on this activity, especially when you add new buttons to the collection regularly.

One Step Further

Once students have sorted the buttons by attribute, encourage them to create patterns such as: red button – blue button – green button – red button – green button . . . .

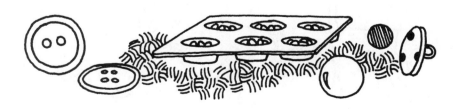

Link to Language

Allow each student to pick a favorite button. Go around the room and ask each student to explain why the button he or she chose is his or her favorite. Perhaps it's the color or the way it feels. Maybe it reminds him of the buttons on his favorite coat or her favorite sweater. Put a piece of thread or yarn through the buttonhole and let students wear their favorite button!

25. Animal Sort

Animals. A high interest topic that's timeless. The math possibilities are endless.

Outcome
Students will sort animals into groups.

Materials
• several plastic animal sets: dogs, whales, monkeys, sea animals, dinosaurs, zoo animals, farm animals, horses, jungle animals, birds, snakes, insects
• several long pieces of yarn

Teacher Prep
No preparation required other than obtaining materials.

Group Activity
Select two animal sets. Mix up all of the plastic animal toys. Lay them out on the table or floor. Create two large, overlapping circles with the yarn. Students pick up one animal at a time and decide where the animal goes: In the left circle? In the right circle? Where the circles intersect? The intersection is the area in which the item has characteristics of both the left and right circles.

One Step Further
Increase the complexity of this activity by making more circles. They can all intersect at a particular point. Add more animal sets, too. For example, a whale would fit into two groups: the whale animal set and the sea animal set. Likewise, the giraffe would be sorted into the zoo and jungle animal sets.

If purchasing the animals sets is too great an expense, use animal clip art! Duplicate, color, cut and laminate.

For older students, animals can be sorted into vertebrates (with backbone) and invertebrates (without backbone), or warm-blooded and cold-blooded.

Link to Science
Animals that have a backbone are classified as either mammals, birds, fish, reptiles or amphibians. Classroom pets provide an opportunity for students to make observations and learn the importance of pet care and responsibility. Adopt a hamster or guinea pig. How about a lizard or frog? Fish are yet another alternative. Discuss the characteristics which make each of these animals unique. Research other animals that fit into these five groups.

26. Pattern Block Graphing

This is a terrific activity for familiarizing students with the shapes and colors represented in a set of pattern blocks.

Outcome
Students will sort pattern blocks according to their shape and color.

Materials
- set of pattern blocks
- portion cup or small paper cup
- paper mat for sorting
- camera (optional)

Teacher Prep
Prepare a sorting mat from poster board or butcher paper. Divide the mat into six columns. Label each column with a different pattern block. The mat can be laminated for durability.

Group Activity
The student scoops a cup full of pattern blocks from the main container of blocks. Upon pouring them onto a table, the student sorts the blocks by shape and color on the sorting mat. Each shape has its own color. For example, triangles are always green; squares are always orange.

The students then count the pattern blocks in each column. This can prompt a variety of discussion points, such as: How many of each shape did you have? What shape did you have more of? Less of?

Students can document this experience by creating a smaller version of the chart on drawing paper, using teacher-made construction paper pattern blocks, pattern block rubber stamps or template, tracing around actual blocks, free-hand drawing of shapes, or taking a photograph of the student next to the product.

One Step Further
Have students repeat this activity several times through the course of a week. Each time they conduct the task be sure the students record their results. Compare the documentation. Ask students if the results from the first experience are the same as in those of the second and third experiences.

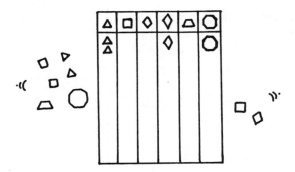

Links to Art and Math
Obtain a box of Froot Loops® cereal, yarn-type sewing needles and some yarn. Have students work in pairs to create cereal patterns on a string. When a pattern has been established and repeated several times, tie the ends of the yarn together to make a wearable, edible manipulative!

27. Frog Sort

This sorting activity will compliment your thematic unit on animals or your literature unit using any of *Frog and Toad Stories* by Arnold Lobel.

Outcome
Students will sort objects according to similar characteristics.

Materials
- several copies of the frog patterns on page 103
- paper to cover and decorate the box
- marking pens of various colors
- paper mat to graph frogs by attribute
- shoe box

Procedure
Prepare several copies of the frog patterns on green paper. Vary the number of each pattern you make. Cover patterns with clear, self-adhesive paper (such as Con-Tact™ paper) or laminate for longevity.

Cover an empty shoe box and lid with butcher paper. Decorate with frog patterns and marking pen. Store frog manipulatives in box.

Create a reusable sorting mat from white butcher paper. Draw lines on the paper to create as many sections a student would need for any one sorting activity. Laminate for durability. The teacher has freedom to change the color of frogs for duplicating patterns on various colors of paper or using marking pens. Size can be altered, smaller or larger, by changing the copy size on the duplicating machine.

Group Activity
After showing students the frog manipulatives, ask them to name the different ways a person could sort the frogs. For younger students, affix one of each type of frog on the butcher paper mat so students will have a starting point. Some ideas for how to sort include the position of the frog, color of skin or size.

FROGS	
Yellow Frogs	Red Frogs
Rainbow Colored Frogs	Big Frogs
Small Frogs	Blue Frogs
Happy Frogs	Sad Frogs

Link to Art
Enlarge one of the frog patterns and duplicate two per student on white or green butcher paper. Either the teacher or student may cut out the frogs. Students can decorate the frogs with paint or crayons.

The teacher lines up the two patterns so their edges match and staples the frog together, approximately a quarter of an inch from the edge. Leave a portion of the frog unstapled and stuff the frog with newspaper. Finish stapling and add large, wiggly eyes to both sides of the paper frog. Suspend them from the ceiling or create a bulletin board with frogs and lily pads!

28. Sticker Stampede

This easy-to-make activity will become a classroom favorite.

Outcome

Students will sort stickers into specific categories.

Materials

- assortment of inexpensive stickers
- 3" x 5" (7.62 x 12.7 cm) index cards
- resealable plastic sandwich bags

Teacher Prep

The preparation for this activity is minimal. Obtain an assortment of stickers such as smiley faces (in a variety of colors), animals, flowers and cartoon characters. Color coding labels are another alternative. The ¾" (1.91 cm) round labels come in a variety of colors including primary colors, white and fluorescents. Place one sticker on each index card. If you are a rubber stamp collector, use stamping images in conjunction with the stickers. Or use the stamps alone with varying colors of ink. Quantities can also be manipulated on each card. The number of cards you make and the amount of sorting categories will vary according to the needs and abilities of your students. Shuffle the cards and store them in a resealable, plastic sandwich bag. Several activity sets can be made to involve as many students as possible.

Group Activity

This task can be done as a whole or small group, with pairs of students or individually. The object is to group cards with similar characteristics together. Students can group stickers by color, object, shape, size or quantity.

If you have enough materials, make additional sets to send home with a note.

29. Flower Power

Your room will bloom with activity as your students become involved with this sorting activity.

Outcome
Students will sort flowers into sets.

Materials
- flower reproducibles below and on page 104
- colored markers
- scissors
- lamination
- yarn

Teacher Prep
Using the patterns provided on this page and page 104, create a reproducible page (illustrated above) and make several copies. Color each of the flowers solid colors, except for three. The petals of those three can be a combination of colors. Laminate the flowers for durability. Cut two pieces of yarn to make a pair of large circles on the floor.

Group Activity
The teacher determines how the flowers should be sorted. There are many options: sort by petal shape, color or size. The yarn circles that are on the floor should overlap. This yarn model is called a Venn diagram. Sets are created within the Venn diagram. The overlapping portion of the circles is the area in which the object possesses both characteristics of the two sets. Students select one flower at a time and place it in the appropriate circle or overlapping portion (intersection).

One Step Further
Create more flowers from the reproducible page you have made. Increase the complexity of the decoration: i.e. patterns on the petals instead of solid colors, sequins in the center (after lamination process), ladybugs and bees on the flowers, etc. Add a third yarn circle to the Venn diagram for a greater sorting challenge! Be sure to create flowers which possess all three characteristics so they can be placed in the intersection!

Enlarge and duplicate

Link to Science
This activity will certainly complement a unit on plants! Decorate your science table to reflect your plant unit: two or three hand lenses; a couple of small, potted, flowering plants; a diagram of the flowering plant; reference books and pictures; and a collection of seeds labeled with the types of plants they represent. Put "Flower Power" in a basket and add it to your display!

30. Rock Collection

Everybody likes rocks. This is a chance to examine them from a math and science point of view!

Outcome
Students will classify rocks according to their properties.

Materials

- 1 rock per student
- egg cartons
- tissue paper
- masking tape and pen
- reference books on rocks and minerals (optional)

Teacher Prep
Send a note home with students several days in advance of this activity. The note can let parents know that you are studying sets and classification in math using rocks. (This lesson also ties in beautifully with science!) Each child should locate and bring to school one rock. The rock should not be expensive or of sentimental value, in the event something happens to it. The teacher should have some "back-up" rocks handy in case a student doesn't bring one to school.

Group Activity
Students should have their rocks placed on the floor or table, right in front of them. On the bottom of each rock, place a piece of masking tape with the student's name (so they can be returned later). Ask students to describe their rocks. These characteristics can be listed on the chalk or marker board.

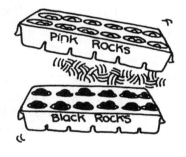

When the list has been completed, ask students what kinds of categories they can make from these words. For example, if students describe their rocks as light or heavy, a category called "weight" could be made. If their rocks are pink, yellow or black, a category called "color" could be made.

After the categories have been discussed and recorded on the board, start with one category (such as color) and ask students to sort their rocks according to that category. Other categories can included hardness (Moh's hardness scale is a popular measuring device), luster (shine) and streaks or speckles.

After sorting the rocks in various ways, select the category which was favored by the group and display them accordingly. Egg cartons, lined with colored tissue paper, make an extremely effective display. If color was the favored category, one egg carton could be labeled "Pink Rocks" and another "Black Rocks," etc., and those rocks fitting the description would be displayed in their specific carton.

Link to Literature
Everybody Needs a Rock by Byrd Baylor (Aladdin Books, 1985) describes ten rules for selecting your own special rock. Check local telephone listings for rock shops in your area. A variety of rocks can be purchased in bulk quantities. Try obtaining several different kinds of small rocks and let students select their own rocks. Then students can tell why they selected the rocks they did.

31. Bean Soup

This hot activity won't burn your tongue!

Outcome
Students will classify beans and sort accordingly.

Materials
- soup pot
- several soup bowls: one for each type of bean
- several varieties of dried beans
- construction paper
- white glue
- crayons or pencils

Teacher Prep
Select several kinds of dried beans. These might include white beans, red beans, pink beans, black-eyed beans or peas, pinto beans, lentils, split peas, kidney beans, navy beans, garbanzo beans or chick peas, and lima beans.

Fold one piece of construction paper for each student into squares–the same number as there are bean types. Glue a different bean in each square. This will let students know which beans go into each box.

When working with younger children, the larger the bean, the better. These children may not have the manual dexterity required to manipulate split peas or lentils. Younger children should also be supervised closely to avoid beans being put into the nose, ears or mouth.

Link to Literature
As a culminating activity, read aloud **Stone Soup** *by Marcia Brown (Aladdin Books, 1975). Send home a note requesting items for a classroom version of stone soup: barley, carrots, cabbage, potatoes, celery, beef or chicken broth, and some seasoning. Slow cook the ingredients in a crock pot. Serve with crackers.*

Group Activity
Mix uncooked beans in the soup pot. Give each student a small bowl of mixed beans and several clean, empty soup bowls. Students are to sort the beans into their respective bowls. When the sorting is complete, each student should then glue the beans in each bowl to the corresponding box on the construction paper. The older the student, the more variety you can add to the soup pot. Challenge students by increasing the actual number of beans used in the activity.

One Step Further
Make a class graph! Record the number of beans each student has in each of the categories. A bar graph would be the most appropriate.

32. "Eggs"act Match

This game is *"eggs"actly* what you need to liven up a unit on eggs or spring!

Outcome
Students will identify similar sets of objects based on numbers and colors.

Materials
- plastic eggs
- small plastic links (such as those made by Learning Resources or Forecees Co.)
- basket to hold eggs

Procedure
Put a predetermined number of links in one egg. For example, five green links. Put another set of five green links into another egg. Continue filling the eggs with varying numbers of links. Be sure to create a "matching" egg with the same number and color features. When all of the eggs have been filled, mix them up in the basket.

Opening Activity
Start a discussion about eggs: Do you like eggs? What can you do with eggs? How can eggs be cooked? What do you like to eat with your eggs? Give students paper plates and crayons and have them draw pictures of their favorite egg dishes. An example might be drawing scrambled eggs (coloring them yellow), bacon strips and buttered toast.

Group Activity
Students can work individually or in pairs as they try to match the eggs which contain the same links. Once students have mastered this game, you can make it more complex by mixing the colors of the links within each egg, as well as the number!

Links to Science and Literature
Watching eggs as they hatch is a phenomenal experience! **The Egg: A First Discovery Book** *by Gallimard Jeunesse and Pascale de Bourgoing (Scholastic: New York, 1989) is a brightly colored picture book with a clever surprise . . . color overlays that, when removed, allow the reader to see inside such things as a chicken and an egg. Try obtaining fertilized chicken eggs and an inexpensive incubator. Discover the wonder of life in your own classroom.*

33. Big, Bigger, Biggest

Hooking the BIG one becomes an exciting challenge with this small group activity.

Outcome
Students will compare objects of differing size and put them in order from small to large.

Materials
- fish pattern (page 103)
- colored markers
- white card stock or construction paper
- small, round magnets (available at craft stores)
- wooden dowel and yarn (for fishing pole)
- 3 small paper buckets (available at paint stores)
- scissors
- tackle box (optional)
- lamination (optional)

Teacher Prep
Enlarge and duplicate several copies of the fish pattern. (You will need to make three different sizes–big, bigger and biggest–for this activity.) Heavy-weight paper is recommended, such as card stock or construction paper. Color the fish with markers. Cut them out and laminate for durability. Glue a round magnet near the mouth of each fish. Make a fishing pole by tying yarn to one end of the wooden dowel. Attach another round magnet to the other end of the yarn.

Group Activity
Students go fishing by dangling the fishing rod near the magnetic fish. As the fish become "attracted" to the line, students can remove the fish and put them in one of three buckets: big, bigger, biggest. Several poles can be made to accommodate larger groups. An infinite number of fish can be duplicated and prepared for this activity. This can also be made into a learning center where students have the freedom to engage in dramatic play!

One Step Further
Add to the complexity of this activity by enlarging and/or reducing the reproducible fish page. You'll also need more paper buckets for students to compare and sort the fish.

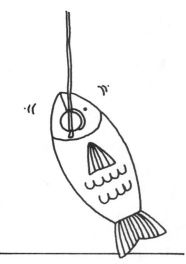

Link to Literature
The Rainbow Fish.
Marcus Pfister. New York: North - South Books, 1992. This book tells of a fish who learns about friendship and sharing.

After reading **The Rainbow Fish** *aloud, have students create their own rainbow fish! Enlarge one of the fish patterns from the Group Activity. Make scissors, glue, markers and aluminum foil available for students to make a school of rainbow fish!*

34. Which Is Heavier?

This measuring activity acts as a precursor to measuring weight in standard units.

Outcome
Students will compare the weight of two objects and will create a "live"graph, recording the findings of the comparison.

Materials
- simple balance
- wooden block (such as a single "unit" hardwood block
- several random items to be compared with wooden block
- long sheet of butcher paper
- marking pen

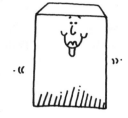

Teacher Prep
Prepare a live graph by drawing a line through the center of the butcher paper lengthwise. Label each column: "Heavier Than" and "Lighter Than."

Collect a variety of items. Some suggestions include several crayons, smaller and larger wooden blocks, foam building pieces, connecting blocks (such as Legos™), small toys, plush toy animals, die-cast cars, plastic dishes, a cup of water, a piece of fruit, a small book. Lay the items in a line, on the floor or table.

Group Activity
Give students time to examine all of the objects. Begin a discussion with students about how we determine the weight of certain things: A piece of fruit? A dog? A person? The answer–scales! A balance is a type of scale. It allows us to compare the weight of two objects or quantities.

Ask students to make a guess (hypothesis) if each object is going to be heavier or lighter than the one unit, hardwood block. Students then conduct the experiment by measuring each object against the one unit block. If the object is lighter, then students can put that item under the "Lighter Than" category of the live graph. Otherwise, the object is put in the "Heavier Than" column.

What happens if the object is *equal* in weight to the unit block? Let students brainstorm as to where they would put the object on the graph. One possible solution may be to put the object "on the line" which separates the two columns.

Link to Social Studies
Some community helpers use scales in their work. Challenge your students to name those community helpers and what their scales measure. Examples might include a grocer who weighs fruit, vegetables, meat and deli foods; a geologist who weighs rocks; a scientist who weighs chemicals and samples; and a nurse who weighs people!

35. Pick a Card

Comparisons are a critical part of our daily lives. Teach it in a fun way using playing cards!

Outcome
Students will compare several cards with one specific card. They will determine if cards drawn randomly are larger or smaller than the one specific card.

Materials
• regular deck of playing cards

Teacher Prep
No preparation required other than obtaining the materials.

Group Activity
Remove the following cards from the deck: Kings, Queens, Jacks and Aces. Shuffle the remaining cards well. Introduce the activity by asking the class to name each of the cards. Select one card by which the rest will be compared, such as the 6♣. Shuffle the cards a second time. Each student draws a card from the top of the deck. The challenge is to decide if the number on the drawn card is larger or smaller than the 6♣. In three cases, the numbers will be the same: 6♠, 6♦ and 6♥.

Repeat this activity by selecting a new card by which the rest will be compared and shuffle the remaining cards.

One Step Further
Students will have fun practicing addition skills through the use of card games. For example, the teacher selects a number (such as 50) and students take turns drawing cards and adding their values together until one of them reaches 50 first! Include the Kings, Queens, Jacks (10 points each) and Aces (11 points each) for an extra challenge. Other possibilities include subtracting the smallest from the largest card or multiplying the cards.

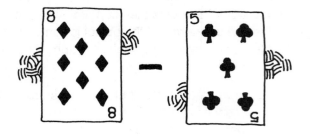

Link to Art
Students can create their own classroom deck of cards! Instead of ♠, ♣, ♥ and ♦, students make up their own suits reflecting a special unit they're studying: i.e. space, animals or parts of speech.

36. Which One Is Greater?

Compare the two numbers and find out!

Outcome

Students will identify numbers 1-100. They will compare two numbers and determine which is greater.

Materials

- deck of number cards from 1-100
- "greater than" symbol (>)
- box of craft sticks

Teacher Prep

If you don't have a set of number cards labeled 1-100, a deck can easily be made with a package of 3" x 5" (7.62 x 12.7 cm) index cards. Cards should be thoroughly shuffled before the final group activity begins. Count and bundle craft sticks in groups of ten.

Group Activity

As a warm-up activity, randomly show students number cards one at a time. As they are shown, select volunteers to identify the number. When you feel students have mastered number identification, do several practice rounds of comparing two numbers.

Introduce the terms *larger, bigger* and *greater than*. These are vocabulary words students will be using throughout the primary and intermediate grades. Select two numbers between 1-20 and hold them up. Ask student volunteers to identify the numbers. Choose two more students to count out craft sticks which represent each of the numbers. Ask the class which number represents the larger, bigger, or greater amount after examining the craft sticks. Numbers in the 10s, 20s, 30s, 40s, 50s, 60s, 70s, 80s, and 90s can be represented (in part) with the bundles of 10 you prepared earlier.

Older students can be introduced to the greater than symbol (>). When a number is placed to the left of this symbol, it means that number is greater than the number on the right side. Using the metaphor "open jaws," have students visualize that the jaws like to "eat" the larger number.

For the final group activity, the cards should be shuffled and placed facedown. Select two students to draw two number cards. Have them show the numbers to the class. Members of the class then volunteer to determine which of the two numbers is larger than the other. Students may use craft sticks as counters to see and compare quantities.

Link to Language

Fold an 18" x 24" (45.72 x 60.96 cm) sheet of construction paper in half. Label the left side "large" and the right side "small." Ask students to find magazine pictures of objects that are large and small, cut them out and mount them on the appropriate side of the paper with glue.

This kind of task requires some critical thinking on the part of students. For example, a car is very big, but compared to a flower on the next page of the magazine, they may look like they are the same size. Decide whether the students will compare and label objects based upon their "literal" appearance in the magazine or their appearance in "reality."

37. Our Classroom Comparison Book

Short, fat, high, low . . . This is how comparisons go!

Outcome
Students will discover relationships between two objects.

Materials
- 9" x 12" (22.86 x 30.48 cm) blank drawing paper
- marking pen
- glue
- construction paper
- yarn
- magazine picture
- uncooked pasta

Teacher Prep
In addition to obtaining the previously mentioned materials, collect other things you have that would enhance this activity.

Write the following comparison words on the blank drawing paper (one per page):

fast	slow
long	short
thin	thick
large	small
hot	cold
high	low

Feel free to add more comparison words to the list. Randomly place the following objects on a table which is accessible to students: a picture of a marathon runner, a picture of a tortoise, a 2" (5.08 cm) piece of yarn, a 12" (30.48 cm) piece of yarn, an uncooked lasagna noodle, an uncooked piece of spaghetti, a magazine picture of a construction vehicle, a magazine picture of a compact or small car, a picture of "steaming" food, a picture of ice cream or a cold drink and two construction paper arrows: one is glued in the "up direction" at the top of a piece of paper, the other is glued in the "down direction" at the bottom of a piece of paper.

Group Activity
The teacher introduces the activity by reviewing the words that describe comparisons: thick–thin, large–small, etc. Students are then paired off. One person from each pair is to select an item from the materials table.

When all of the items have been claimed, arrange students in a semicircle and discuss the objects. Ask students to find an object that someone else has that is similar, yet different. For example, the pieces of yarn are similar in terms of the material, yet different in length. When the length of the yarn is compared, we see one piece is long, the other is short. When the objects have been compared and matched, the second student in the pair glues the object to the corresponding paper labeled with the comparison word. Punch holes in the paper and use binder rings to keep the pages together!

Link to Drama
Goldilocks and the Three Bears *is a classic children's story that focuses on comparisons. Read this story aloud to your students (there are many versions), then divide the class into small groups. Have each group reenact the story. Don't forget the props: 3 graduated sizes of bowls, chairs and beds (pictures of beds will do)!*

38. Boxes, Boxes and More Boxes!

Children *love* boxes! They hold so many things, including this math activity!

Outcome
Students will compare boxes and their attributes.

Materials
• wide variety of boxes

Teacher Prep
Start collecting boxes well in advance of this project. You may want to ask parents to save boxes they might have around the house. Boxes can also be obtained from "box shops," department stores, grocery stores, shoe stores and jewelry stores. Depending on the size of the boxes, you may want to store the boxes in one large, decorated box. If possible, get an appliance box (refrigerator, washer or dryer). The mere size of the box will excite children!

Group Activity
Lay all of the boxes out for students to handle and examine. If there are enough boxes, have each student select one. Students then take turns describing the physical features of the box, what the box is used for and what else could fit in the box.

Return the boxes to a central area, where they can be easily seen and are accessible to children. The teacher then poses a series of questions for students to answer. In many cases there may be more than one answer. Accept any answer that can be justified.

1. Holding any box, the teacher asks, "Show me another box that is larger (or smaller) than the one I'm holding.

2. Show me a box that is the same size and shape as the one I'm holding.

3. Show me a box that is deeper than the one I'm holding.

4. Show me a box that feels heavier than the one I'm holding."

One Step Further
Use the boxes for sets and classifying! Allow students to decide the categories they will use to sort the boxes. They can work as a class, in small groups or pairs.

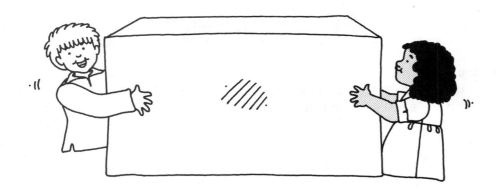

Link to Literature
*Learn to make an airplane, dinosaur or car with **Build It with Boxes** by Joan Irvine (Beech Tree, 1993). There are also several ideas on how to make boxes utilizing paper folding techniques. The book is intended for children 10 and up, however this is a must have book for any teacher's personal resource library.*

39. Hot or Cold?

Which is hot, chicken soup or a chocolate shake?

Outcome
Students will compare items relating to hot and cold.

Materials
- magazine pictures or photographs of hot and cold items such as a cup of hot chocolate, a soda with ice, a Popsicle™, a bowl of soup, a milk shake, a piece of pizza, steamed vegetables and a gallon of ice cream

  In addition to pictures, bring to class "the real thing": a box of frozen peas, a frozen dinner and a basket of hot rolls.

Teacher Prep
After obtaining various pictures from the Materials list, you may want to mount them on poster board and laminate for durability. These pictures can also become part of a picture file teachers create for use in other class activities.

Group Activity
Engage students in a discussion about hot and cold. Questions you might pose are

1. What kinds of things remind you of *hot*?
2. What kinds of things remind you of *cold*?
3. When it is really cold outside, what do you wear?
4. When it is really hot outside, what do you wear?
5. What are the things you do when it is cold outside?
6. What are the things you do when it is hot outside?

Distribute two pictures of food items randomly to each student. Go around the room and ask students to *compare* the two pictures, then ask which food is *hot*. There are three choices for answers: One of the two pictures shows a hot food, both of the pictures show hot foods, neither of the pictures shows hot foods. When everyone has had a turn, mix the pictures up, redistribute them, and then ask which food is *cold*.

One Step Further
Create a two-column graph from butcher paper. Label the headings "Hot Foods" and "Cold Foods." Have students put their food pictures (or the actual item) in the correct column.

Link to Think About
Can some foods that are traditionally served hot, be eaten cold and vice versa? Can you name some?

40. Comparing Fruits

This math experience would be a terrific closing activity for a unit on health or nutrition!

Outcome
Students will use a nonstandard measuring device to determine the sizes of various fruits. They will graph and compare results and draw conclusions from those results.

Materials
- selection of fruits: watermelon, pumpkin, cantaloupe, honeydew, guava, apple, orange, pear, pomegranate, grape, papaya, tangerine, apricot, peach, casaba, strawberry, raspberry, blueberry, mango, lemon, lime
- ball of dark-colored yarn
- scissors
- piece of butcher paper
- colored marker

Teacher Prep
Across the bottom of the butcher paper, list the names of the fruits being measured. Decide how the fruits will be measured: by height or width. All pieces of fruit will be measured in the same way. During the measuring, students may require teacher or peer assistance. An alternative to working individually is to pair students in such a way that their skills complement one another.

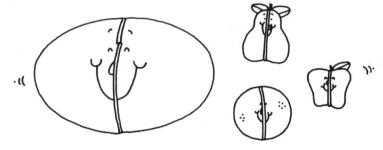

Group Activity
Demonstrate for students the way in which they will measure their fruits. This can be done by wrapping the yarn around the fruit horizontally or vertically, and cutting the yarn where the end meets the beginning.

Students then glue their pieces of yarn to the butcher paper chart, where the names of the fruits appear. When all of the fruits have been measured, ask students what they can tell from the information on the chart. For example: The apple is much smaller than the watermelon. The apple is much larger then the blueberry.

Photograph the students during the measuring activity, when they glue their pieces of yarn and a picture of the final graph. Have the students stand behind the chart so they are included in the picture!

One Step Further
If the fruits were measured horizontally, now measure them vertically. Is there a difference in the measurement? Try this activity with vegetables. What kinds of conclusions can be drawn when comparing fruits and vegetables?

Link to Social Studies
Friendship salad is a popular recipe that fosters good feelings by all who participate! First, the teacher (or supervising adult) cuts up the fruits into manageable pieces. (Note: Students should not be allowed to use any knife other than plastic for safety reasons!) Students can then practice their cutting skills using a plastic knife. Give everyone a chance to cut the fruits and put them into a large mixing bowl. Chill and serve the friendship salad. Take a group photograph of students preparing or eating. Send duplicated copies home with the caption "Friendship Salad" and the date on the back.

41. Block City

Future architects cooperate and create in this very developmentally appropriate activity.

Outcome
Students will identify and use geometric solids to build an imaginary city.

Materials
- variety of wooden blocks–half units, units, double units, quadruple units, pillars, floor boards (the aforementioned are rectangular prisms); cylinders, curves; triangles, ramps; and switches
- large area on the floor
- accessories: figures (i.e. animals and people), vehicles, furniture, road signs, trees, etc.

To the Teacher
Blocks are an essential part of the early childhood curriculum. Through block play, children derive meaning of the world around them. The applications tap into such areas as math, science, social studies, art, language and dramatic play.

Blocks can be costly, yet it's an investment that stands the test of time and durability. An economical approach may involve a gradual acquisition, such as 6-12 blocks every month or two. It also pays to shop around. Some stores offer starter sets at very reasonable prices.

Space figures are those that occupy more than one plane. You might be more familiar with the term *3-D* (three-dimensional). These figures include cubes, pyramids, spheres, cones, cylinders and rectangular prisms. Depending upon the ability of your students, this information may or may not be appropriate at this time.

Teacher Prep
No preparation required other than obtaining materials.

Link to Literature
Color Zoo. *Lois Ehlert. HarperCollins, 1989. Take a unique look at zoo animals through the use of color and shape. Students can add a "zoo" to their block city. A set of plastic zoo animals would be the finishing touch!*

Opening Activity
Collect several different blocks as described in the Materials list. Ask student volunteers to select a block that looks like:

1. a long rectangle
2. a short rectangle
3. a large triangle
4. a small triangle
5. a round shape

Discuss as a group how some shapes can be arranged to form similar shapes. For example, two smaller triangles put together make a larger triangle. Put them together in yet another way and you have a square!

Next, talk about the kinds of things you might see in a city: buildings, streets and highways, traffic lights and signs, and people. Tell students they will work together to build a city of their own. Let each student decide what he or she will build or help build. When everyone knows their "job," send them on their way!

Group Activity

After providing ample floor space, encourage students to engage in some experimental architecture! There is no right or wrong way of doing things. Students can also be reminded of an important rule for cooperative play: Respect the work of others. By providing students with the accessories (also mentioned under Materials), this dramatic play opportunity becomes greatly enhanced. Be sure to document this experience by taking lots of photographs.

42. Shapes Around Us

Discover the world of shapes by examining common objects all around us!

Outcome
Students will identify the basic shapes that exist in our environment.

Materials

- black construction paper
- scissors
- camera with color film

To the Teacher

An important aspect of this activity is observational skills. Specifically, students will need to examine the form of objects and make comparisons. For example, a traffic signal is rectangular and the individual lights on the rectangle are circles.

Students should have some practice with shapes before being expected to identify them in common objects. This can be done by introducing flannel board stories, where the characters are actually shapes. Cindy Circle, Ramon Rectangle, Squeaky Square and Tracy Triangle can appear in a series of ongoing adventures. Perhaps they encounter more characters with more complex shapes: Polly Polygon, Sven Sphere or Carmen Cube.

Teacher Prep

From the black construction paper, cut the following shapes: circle, rectangle, square and triangle. The shapes should be large. Load the camera with color film before your walking field trip.

Group Activity

After assembling the students, introduce the construction paper shapes one at a time. Ask students to describe the shapes. For example, a circle is round, a square has four equal sides, a triangle has three sides and a rectangle has two sets of parallel lines and four right (or 90°) angles. Most students should not be expected to be so precise. Common descriptions of rectangles would include "four-sided," and "longer or wider than a square." A square is also known as a rectangle. The difference is the square has equal sides.

When students have displayed an understanding of the basic shapes, ask for volunteers to name items in the classroom that have a circular, triangular, rectangular or square-like shape. As soon as you and the students feel comfortable, move outdoors and select things in nature and the city which possess the characteristics of circles, triangles, rectangles and squares. Take photographs of students posing among the "shapes around us." Create a classroom bulletin board with four sections, one for each shape. After the photos have been developed, allow students to help in displaying them in the proper area of the bulletin board.

Link to Social Studies

Encourage parents/care-givers to select an item from home with their child that has the characteristics of a circle, square, triangle or rectangle. It may be a book, a towel, a gift box or a lollipop. Set aside time the next morning for students to discuss the item they brought to school and its shape.

43. Shape Books

Outcome

Students will make shape books using their knowledge of geometric figures, make comparisons between shapes and use language in reinforcing math concepts.

Materials

- several sheets of 8½" x 11" (21.59 x 27.94 cm) white paper per student
- several sheets of colored construction paper
- scissors
- glue
- pencil or colored marker
- stapler

To the Teacher

It's important that students learn math through a variety of experiences, not just during "math time." This activity combines math concepts with language skills.

Teacher Prep

If students aren't able to cut shapes from paper, the teacher may want to cut several construction paper shapes in various colors from which students can choose. The teacher will also take dictation from students as pages are completed if students are unable to write or use inventive spelling.

Group Activity

Assemble students in a circle to review the basic shapes: circle, square, triangle and rectangle. This may involve the "naming" of a shape when it is shown, a description of the shape, or objects in the environment which contain the shape being shown.

This activity will be most effective if done in small groups over a period of several days. Students will create one or two pages per day with help from the teacher, aide or parent volunteer. A shape book format is suggested below. This should in no way limit other ideas the teacher may wish to implement.

Cover page—Decorated in a collage fashion, students can cut and glue shapes from construction paper, wallpaper sample books, magazines or newspapers.

Pages 1-4—Each page is decorated with one large basic shape. Students can dictate the name of the shape ("This is a square"), the color of the shape ("This is a green square") and the size of the shape ("This is a big square"), etc.

Pages 5-9—Each page is decorated with more than one of the same shape. For example, page 5 may have two green squares, one large green square and one small orange square. The dictation should gradually become more complex.

For added novelty, have students select their favorite shape. Trim the book cover and pages to look like a "square book," "triangle book," "rectangle book" or "circle book."

Link to Large Motor Skills

Create shapes with the help of your students. Instruct the class to form a large circle. This can be done by joining hands, moving back slowly, then letting all hands drop to the sides.

Create the other basic shapes in the same manner. When students have mastered this physical task, increase the difficulty by suggesting the formation of 2 or 3 circles simultaneously! These activities lend themselves to cooperation without competition.

44. Shape Scavenger Hunt

Shapes are found in everything, especially items around the house.

Outcome
Students will locate shapes in everyday objects. They will trace around shapes.

Materials
- kitchen objects: plastic storage containers of different shapes and sizes, jars, pots and pans, plates, cups, canned food items, cereal boxes, utensils, plastic bottles, etc.
- bathroom items: box of tissues, toilet paper, bar of soap, empty shampoo bottle, box of bandages, makeup caddy, comb, etc.
- construction paper
- crayons or pencils

Teacher Prep
Collect suggested kitchen and bathroom items. Place kitchen items on one table, bathroom items on another. Label each table with a sign "Things We Find in the Kitchen" and "Things We Find in the Bathroom."

Opening Activity
Discuss with your class all of the different objects a person can find in a house. Go room by room. For example, in the living room there might be a television, lamp, table and sofa. Then talk about the shape of these objects. Some tables are rectangular, circular, square and oval. If there is a dollhouse or housekeeping center in your classroom, borrow the necessary items being discussed to point out where these shapes are located. Students can also discuss objects within the classroom and the shapes they have!

Group Activity
Equip students with a piece of construction paper and a crayon or pencil. Tell students you have selected some items from home that have certain shapes. Ask for student volunteers to name the object and the shape that is found in the object. Students can select whatever objects they would like to use, and trace around the object on construction paper. For example, a bottle has a circular shape on the bottom which students can trace. Large kitchen spoons have a kind of oval shape. Instant oatmeal comes in rectangular packages and a cylinder.

Note About Safety: Do not select items which might compromise the safety of your students. This includes ingestible things like mouthwash, bleach, hydrogen peroxide, etc. Better to use *empty* containers that have been thoroughly cleaned out.

Link to Science and Health

While studying objects found in the kitchen, whip out the cookbook and find a simple recipe to make with students. Noncook recipes may be easiest, such as punch or lemonade, cheese sandwiches or peanut butter and celery.

Items from the bathroom may spark a conversation about hygiene: proper flossing and brushing of teeth, washing your hands and face and combing your hair.

45. Get into Shape

This activity will prove to be quite a workout for everyone!

Outcome
Students will work cooperatively to form shapes as a group.

Materials
• camera or video recorder

To the Teacher
Some of the shape vocabulary may be unfamiliar to you. A **right triangle** is a three-sided figure that has one 90° angle. An **isosceles triangle** is a triangle in which two of the three sides are the same size. A **scalene triangle** is a triangle with no two sides being the same size. An **obtuse triangle** is a triangle in which one of the angles is more than 90° but less than 180°. An **acute triangle** is a triangle in which the angles formed are less than 90°. An **equilateral triangle** has three sides and angles which are the same size. If other terms are unclear, a standard college dictionary may come in handy!

Teacher Prep
Review the shapes students have been introduced to, such as right triangle, isosceles triangle, obtuse triangle, acute triangle, scalene triangle, equilateral triangle, pentagon, hexagon, octagon, decagon, square, rectangle, rhombus, trapezoid, circle, semicircle and oval. Have student volunteers draw each shape on the chalk or marker board.

Group Activity
This activity requires the participation of everyone! If your classroom is too small, move the group outside. Explain to the class they will be standing together in various positions to form each of the shapes they have been studying. Ask a student to name a shape, for example, circle. Students would get together, perhaps taking the hand of the person next to them. When everyone has another's hand, students slowly back out and drop hands. For younger students, the teacher can draw the shape on the ground with chalk as a guide. Photograph or videotape the activity, and use it during another shape review!

One Step Further
Make the activity more difficult by suggesting students change the *size* of the shape or by creating several shapes at one time and *intersecting*.

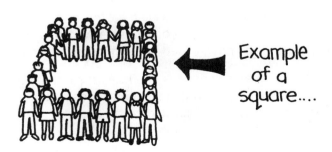

Example of a square....

Link to Physical Education
Have a race! Write each of the shapes on index cards and shuffle well. Divide the class into two groups. Draw the first two cards, tell each group the name of the shape they'll form, then "on your mark, get set, GO!" Time the groups. After several rounds, the group who has accumulated the shortest time wins. Fancy ribbons made from the basic shapes can be awarded to the winning group. Reward everyone in the two groups with stickers or a glass of cold punch.

46. Shape Mates

Can you find the mate to three triangles?

Outcome

Students will reinforce their knowledge of shapes and use memory to match pairs of cards with identical quantities and shapes.

Materials

- set of 30 3" x 5" (7.62 x 12.7 cm) index cards
- set of colored markers

Teacher Prep

Select 30 blank index cards. The teacher makes two cards of each design using a red marker, such as:

> First and second cards: one triangle
> Third and fourth cards: two triangles
> Fifth and sixth cards: three triangles

Continue this pattern of one, two and three shapes for each of the following: circles, squares, stars and half circles. There should be a total of six cards representing each type of shape. Shuffle the 30 cards well.

Group Activity

Demonstrate how Shape Mates is played in front of the class. This could be best accomplished by assembling students around a large table.

Lay the cards out facedown in six groups of five. Select a card and turn it over. Select another card and turn it over. If the two cards are identical, the player then keeps the pair of cards and the next person takes his or her turn. *Identical* means "the same shape and quantity on both cards." If the cards that have been turned over do not match, both cards must then be placed facedown in their original places, and the next player takes his or her turn. The person who has accumulated the most cards at the end of the game wins.

One Step Further

Increase the challenge by matching cards in an entirely different way. This time a "match" will consist of three cards, not two. Example: Match the one, two and three triangle cards. The shape is being matched in a sequence, not an identical match.

Another variation is to create another deck of 30 cards, same shape and quantities but different color (for example, green rather than red shapes). Students can then match pairs that are identical in shape, quantity and color.

Link to Science

Create a matching game that compliments your current science theme. Animals, space, senses, seasons and weather are some examples. Use magazine pictures, clip art, stickers or rubber stamps to make the desired images on the index cards. A smaller, scaled down version of the game can be sent home with directions so students can play the game at home with their families!

47. Pattern Block Puzzles

These are puzzles everyone will enjoy!

Outcome
Students will use problem-solving skills to arrange pattern blocks to fit into a larger shape.

Materials
- set of pattern blocks
- plain sheet of white paper
- black, fine-tip marking pen

Teacher Prep
Select a variety of pattern blocks and arrange them on a sheet of white paper. Each piece should be touching another piece. There should not be any space between the pieces. Once you have decided upon the arrangement, trace around the outer edge of the entire puzzle. This should be one continuous line that ends where you started. Remove the pieces. The puzzle can now be laminated and used repeatedly, or it can be duplicated for individuals.

Group Activity
This activity can be done in small groups, pairs or individually. The objective is to fill in the puzzle with pattern blocks. The outer edges of the blocks must line up precisely with the edge of the puzzle. The pieces must be touching each other with no space between them. There can be numerous solutions to the puzzle.

After students have laid out the pieces, encourage them to go back and trace around each pattern block. Finally, students can color in the pattern block tracings to correspond with the actual blocks.

One Step Further
These puzzles can range from very simple to quite challenging! Create a new puzzle each week for your students. Display the students' solutions. The same activity can be done using tangrams and pentominoes!

Idea for a puzzle...

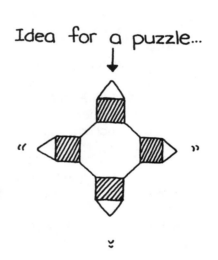

Links to Science and Language
Discuss some of the things that "puzzle" students. For example, "Why is the sky blue?" and "What is lightning?" Make a class book titled "Things That Puzzle Us." Encourage students to ask questions about things they can't explain or don't understand. Your local public library and reference books (encyclopedias, almanacs and dictionaries) are good places to search for answers if you don't have them! Students can dictate their questions to the teacher. The teacher records each question on a sheet of drawing paper, and the students illustrate the pages.

48. SymmeTREE

What a great project for Arbor Day or Johnny Appleseed's birthday!

Outcome
Students will finish drawing and coloring the mirror image of a tree provided by the teacher.

Materials
- tree pattern below
- various colors of green construction paper
- scissors
- white construction paper
- glue
- crayons

To the Teacher
The line of symmetry refers to the place at which an object or shape is divided, where the opposite side is the exact mirror image of the other. A symmetrical figure refers to an object or shape that when divided has two exact matching pairs.

Teacher Prep
Reproduce the tree pattern on green construction paper.

Group Activity
Pair students so each one will get half a tree. Select one of the two students to cut the tree on the dotted line. Students will then glue their half to a piece of white construction paper.

Using a green crayon, students should draw the other half of the tree to make a whole. Brown crayon can be used over the green construction paper (and the white) to illustrate the trunk. The drawings should be as close to a "mirror image" as possible. Display finished projects on a bulletin board labeled "SymmeTREES."

One Step Further
Create apples for your trees with a small apple paper punch or a regular single-hole punch and red paper. Students can put apples on each side of the trees in a symmetrical pattern. (The left side should be a mirror image of the right side.)

Link to Science
*Did you know the edible fruit of an apple tree is called a "pome"? Share this bit of trivia with your class. The word **pome** introduces another topic: "homophones." Homophones are words that sound the same but have different meanings and usually different spellings. Ask your students if they can think of another word that sounds like **pome** but is spelled differently and has another meaning. (The answer is **poem**. This word has the same letters as **pome**; they're simply in a different order!)*

Enlarge and duplicate

Infinite Patterns

The possibilities are endless with this symmetry activity.

Outcome

Students will create symmetrical designs using pattern blocks.

Materials

- set of pattern blocks
- hand-held mirror

Teacher Prep

No preparation required other than obtaining materials.

Group Activity

This activity works very well in small groups or as an individual learning center. Introduce this activity by reviewing the meaning of *line of symmetry* and *symmetrical* (see "SymmeTREE" activity).

Demonstrate on the table one way of arranging pattern blocks. When you have finished, hold the mirror to one side of the design. Direct students to look in the mirror. The reflection or "mirror image" is the next step in completing the symmetrical design. Ask student volunteers to select pattern blocks and place them on the table adjacent to the first design, as seen in the mirror.

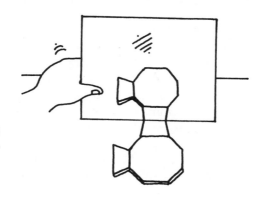

Document the experience by taking photographs of the students in several phases of the activity. Be sure to photograph them with their final products.

Older students can trace around each piece with a pencil and color in the design to match the colors of the actual blocks.

One Step Further

There are lots of variations to this pattern block activity! Limit the types of blocks used, such as only squares and triangles. Establish a minimum and maximum number of blocks that can be used. Students can select a predetermined number of blocks and find all of the different ways the blocks can be arranged that yield a symmetrical design.

Links to Language and Science

Engage students in a discussion about mirrors: Where are they found? (Clothing stores, ophthalmologist's and dentist's offices, in the home, on cars, on telescopes and microscopes, etc.) How do they help us? Incorporate the study of mirrors with a science unit on light.

50. Tell Me a Tangram Story

Use tans to facilitate storytelling! After reading *Grandfather Tang's Story* to your students, let their imaginations and creativity run wild.

Outcome
Students will experiment to create their own figures from tans.

Materials
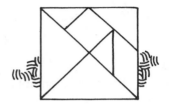
• *Grandfather Tang's Story* by Ann Tompert
• set of tangrams for each student
• overhead projector
• pencils, paper and crayons for students

Procedure
Before reading the story to students, prepare a set of tangrams for each student. This can be done in several ways: purchase bulk sets of manufactured, plastic tangrams, cut tangrams from a manufactured device (i.e. Ellison Letter Machine) or trace around tans (individual pieces) and cut out pieces by hand.

Practice making the tangram animals Tompert presents in her book on the overhead projector. As you read aloud *Grandfather Tang's Story* to your class, either you or an assistant can demonstrate the animal tangrams on the overhead projector using overhead tangrams.

Tompert provides a beautiful explanation of tangrams: what they are and how they are used. This can be used as background information as you prepare students to create their own tangram stories.

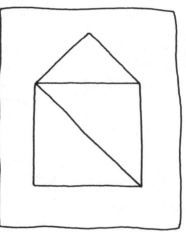

(Tangram picture of a house.)

Each student needs a set of tangrams, paper, pencil and crayons. Students should be encouraged to experiment and form tan pictures of their own. When they have designed a picture to their liking, make the product of their efforts permanent by either you or the student tracing around the shapes on paper and coloring them in.

Alternative
Students can use construction paper tans and glue their final product to paper.

Link to Language
Have students tell stories about their tan character or object. Let students dictate the story to you as you document it on paper or tape-record their stories.

51. Shape-Maker

Shape up with geoboard exercises!

Outcome

Students will make basic shapes on the geoboard with rubber bands. They will perform tasks reinforcing simple geometry and vocabulary.

Materials

- 1 geoboard for every one or two students
- rubber bands
- overhead projector (optional)
- geoboard for the overhead projector (optional)

To the Teacher

Geoboards are a tool used to introduce and reinforce concepts pertaining to geometry. For young children, this includes the properties of shapes, how shapes are formed and the relationship between shapes. Geoboards are available commercially. They commonly contain 25 "pegs." An inexpensive alternative is using brass fasteners and railroad board. As with any new manipulative, it's important that students have an opportunity to explore freely. Be sure to dedicate a day or class period to free exploration. On day two, students will feel more confident about approaching introductory concepts!

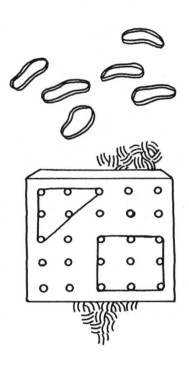

Teacher Prep

No preparation required.

Group Activity

Challenge individuals or pairs of students to create the following shapes on their geoboards: square, rectangle and triangle. Go around the class and ask students to hold up their shapes for others to see. Students can compare shapes with each other. For example, some squares may be smaller than others. There are also a variety of triangles one can make with the geoboard: isosceles, equilateral and right, to name a few.

Other challenges can include:

- Overlap the square and triangle.
- Overlap the square, triangle and rectangle.
- Create two squares that share one side.
- Create a square and triangle that share only one point.
- Design a shape that is symmetrical.
- Design a shape and show how it would look if it were solid.
- What would the design look like if it were flipped? Turned?

Link to Math

Through further experimentation, see how many different sizes and shapes you can design. Can you make a six-sided figure? An eight-sided figure? A ten-sided figure? How about a parallelogram? How many different polygons can you make? Tricky words? Grab a dictionary and go to work!

52. Foiled Shapes

This activity "touches" math, science, social studies and language arts.

Outcome
Students will create impressions of shapes on aluminum foil sheets.

Materials
- 1 sheet of aluminum foil per student
- several cardboard shapes: circles, ovals, various triangles, rectangles, squares, hexagons, octagons, decagons, etc.
- construction paper
- glue

Teacher Prep
From lightweight cardboard, cut several small and large-sized shapes. Several shape impressions can be made on one sheet of foil. The teacher may want to introduce one shape at a time using this activity, or combine the shapes for a culminating activity.

Group Activity
Done in small groups, this activity focuses on tactile learners. The teacher can demonstrate by placing a cardboard shape under the foil, then tracing the edges of the shape with the figure. Light pressure from the finger on the foil will create an impression of the shape(s).

Foil impressions can then be mounted on colored construction paper. A small dab of white glue on each corner of the foil is all that's needed for it to adhere to the construction paper. Matting the foil impression is another display option.

One Step Further
Don't waste those cardboard shapes! When you're finished, have students wrap them with any leftover aluminum foil. Poke a hole in the top of each foiled shape, and suspend them from the ceiling or a wire coat hanger with fishing line. You'll have a dazzling display that teaches!

Link to Science
Aluminum presents a lot of teaching opportunities. Collect aluminum cans for a classroom recycling project and calculate the accumulated weight and money earned. Check with your local recycling center for educational materials. Some facilities offer detailed posters of the recycling process and coupons for teachers. Obtain several items that are made from aluminum, such as pie tins, frozen food packaging, a sample of aluminum siding and window frames. Share these things with your class.

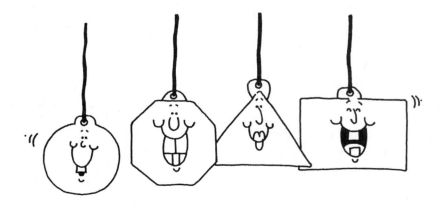

53. Shape Architect

This inexpensive manipulative will provide hours of entertainment.

Outcome
Students will create figures using toothpicks.

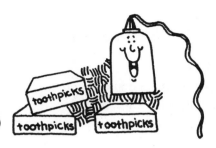

Materials
- several boxes of colored toothpicks
  (Younger students may use craft sticks.
  You can color them with markers if you wish.)
- white construction paper
- glue

Teacher Prep
No preparation required other than obtaining materials.

Opening Activity
Review with the class all of the different shapes that can be made with straight lines: various triangles, rectangles and squares. Ask student volunteers to draw these shapes on the board. Write the name of the shape underneath each one.

Group Activity
Students should be seated around the work tables with supplies located in the center of the table. Challenge students to experiment with the toothpicks and create shapes that have been discussed in the opening activity. The size of the shapes can be increased by doubling the toothpicks used to make each side. Make shapes that are large and small, or shapes that are big, bigger and biggest (math concept: comparing).

When students are comfortable with the shapes they have made, have them glue the toothpick arrangements to the construction paper. Enough room should be left to label the shapes.

By using colored toothpicks, students can reinforce color concepts with shapes: red square, red rectangle, red right triangle, green polygon, extra-large green square, green equilateral triangle.

One Step Further
Primary grade students can be introduced to the concept of perimeter. Perimeter involves adding all of the sides together. Mount toothpick shapes on construction paper flash cards, and label each side with a number. Write number sentences and answers on the back of each card.

Link to Art
With the leftover toothpicks, let students make their own designs, patterns and pictures. Yellow toothpicks can be arranged to make the rays of the sun. Toothpicks placed over a magazine picture of a bear could illustrate a caged animal.

54. What Can You Make?

By themselves, they're just shapes. Put them all together and this is what you've got . . . .

Outcome
Students will use basic shapes to create a picture.

Materials
- various colors of construction paper
- shape stencils or traceables
- pencil
- scissors
- glue
- crayons or colored markers

Teacher Prep
Using shape stencils or objects which can be traced, create various shapes of different sizes and colors. Depending upon the ability, students can cut around the shapes with help or by themselves. Glue and crayons should be on the work tables. Each student needs one piece of white construction paper on which to glue the shapes.

Opening Activity
Take students on a walk around your school. Ask them what kinds of shapes they see in common objects: table, door and display case (rectangular); clock (circular); rubber mat under swing set (square); etc.

After the walk, return to the classroom. Assemble students in a circle by the chalkboard. Ask students to come to the board and draw familiar objects (not limited to outdoors) using rectangles, circles, squares and triangles.

Group Activity
Ask students to return to their work tables. Explain to the group that they will make a picture using basic shapes. The opening activity is important as a brainstorming technique that stimulates higher thinking skills. Allow verbal interaction between students. Collaboration is important! Students should place the shapes on the white construction paper as they want them permanently, then they can glue the shapes down. Create details with crayons or markers. When students finish the project, ask them to describe their pictures to you. Write down what they describe on the back of the pictures.

Link to Language
Cut various sizes and colors of shapes from felt (available at craft and fabric stores). Using a flannel board, ask student volunteers to select felt shapes and make pictures for the class. The group can take turns guessing what the pictures are. Another suggestion: Have students tell a story about the objects or pictures made with the felt shapes!

55. Shape Tracers

Students can extend their knowledge of simple shapes by discovering their importance in other areas of math.

Outcome
Students will reinforce their knowledge of shapes and will compare sizes of shapes.

Materials
- lightweight poster board: red, white, blue, green and yellow
- ruler
- compass
- pencils
- utility knife (**Note:** Only to be used by an adult and with extreme care!)
- single-hole paper punch
- binder rings
- blank, white drawing paper

Teacher Prep
Cut the red poster board into three, 5" x 5" (12.7 x 12.7 cm) pieces (per student). Do the same for the white, blue, green and yellow poster board. Using a ruler, draw one, small equilateral triangle (all three sides are equal in length) on the first piece of red poster board. Draw a slightly larger equilateral triangle on the second one. Draw an even larger triangle on the third. In this way you create a set of graduated stencils!

Create three graduated circle stencils from the white poster board (a compass may come in handy), three graduated rectangle stencils from the blue poster board, three graduated square stencils from the green poster board and a third set of graduated figures (i.e. heart, star, etc.) from the yellow.

Using a utility knife (BE VERY CAREFUL!), cut out each of the shapes from the poster board pieces. Ideal cutting surfaces include a large piece of glass or an acrylic cutting board. The pieces of poster board that have "holes" in them are the stencils. Punch a hole in the top left corner of each stencil and attach them to a binder ring.

Group Activity
This activity is very appropriate for small groups of students or individuals. Distribute the white drawing paper, pencils and sets of stencils. Demonstrate for students how to trace around the inside of the shape pieces. Encourage students to try on their own. They may also want to use crayons or markers to color in the shapes. Ask students to point to each set of shapes: first to the largest, next to the middle sized and finally to the smallest.

Sort and classify all of the large and small shape stencils, or sort the stencils in which the shapes have four sides. Add any new shapes or symbols to the stencil pack.

Link to Art
Divide the class into five groups. Give each group a sheet of white butcher paper. The first group will make a large, red triangle. The second group, a white circle (outlined in black). The third group, a blue rectangle. The fourth group, a green square. The fifth group, a yellow figure. Display them in prominent places around your school with a sign crediting the work to "The Students of Room _____."

56. Magazine Picture Puzzles

No longer is the idea of "pieces" a perplexing puzzle.

Outcome
Students will examine parts of a puzzle and arrange them to create a whole.

Materials
- large, colorful magazine pictures
- construction paper
- scissors
- glue
- plastic, resealable sandwich bags
- lamination for durability (optional)

To the Teacher
The concept of parts and whole is the child's first step on the road to fractions. It's important that students build a foundation of understanding with respect to parts and whole in order to progress to more difficult fractions. This section deals with the idea that pieces put together make a whole, and that a whole is the sum of its parts. The section on fractions, which appears later in this book, will address halves, thirds and fourths.

Teacher Prep
Accumulate pictures from magazines. Natural history, pets and animals, plants and food magazines usually have big, bright, bold pictures that are perfect for this activity. Trim away any parts which detract from the picture. Glue the picture to construction paper and laminate for durability. Cut the picture into pieces. The number of pieces will be determined by the ability of your students and the challenges you're comfortable providing without excessive frustration. Each student should have a puzzle to work on, even if it's only a two-piece puzzle. Store each puzzle in a plastic, resealable bag. Puzzle bags can be kept in a decorated shoe box where puzzles might normally be stored. Picture collection should be an ongoing "hobby." Not only can you constantly provide new puzzles with varying degrees of difficulty, but the pictures come in handy as visuals for special units or other activities!

Group Activity
Discuss with the class how *whole* things can be divided. Ask for student volunteers to name such things. Common responses may include apples, oranges, a soda, a pie or a cookie. Sets of things can also be divided, such as a bucket of die-cast cars, a jar of hard candy or a basket of sandbox toys.

Show the class a completed, cardboard or wooden puzzle. Ask students what they notice about the puzzle. Perhaps it shows someone or thing. It has many pieces. Remove one piece. Is the puzzle still complete or whole? What happens when you put the piece back?

Give each pair of students a magazine puzzle. When the pairs are confident in making the magazine picture whole, let each student select a puzzle from the shoe box to do individually.

Link to Social Studies

Show students an unopened box of crackers. Explain the box represents a whole. Allow each student to take a "piece" of the whole (a cracker). Ask the class if the box of crackers is still the same as it was before it was opened. Then ask students what could be done to make the box "whole" again.

57. Putting It All Together

Whether it's Mr. Potato Head™, a thermos or a board game, they all have parts that make them whole!

Outcome
Students will learn that parts together make a whole.

Materials

- Mr. Potato Head™ toy
- diagram of the human body*
- drawing paper and crayons

Teacher Prep
No preparation required.

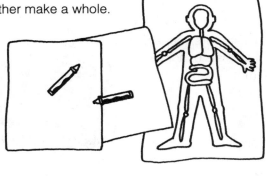

Group Activity
Show students Mr. Potato Head™ unassembled. Discuss the many parts Mr. Potato Head™ has. Ask student volunteers to approach the display area and select a part and name it. Students then add the parts to Mr. Potato Head™. Continue in this fashion until Mr. Potato Head™ is fully assembled. Refer the class to the diagram of the human body. Ask students to point and name the parts they see on the diagram.

Other objects that have parts, which together make them whole include cars, refrigerators and board games. Encourage students to give examples of other things that are made up of several parts.

After the discussion, tell students to return to their seats and draw pictures of themselves "whole."

One Step Further
Set up a display table with the title "The Pieces Put Together Make Us Whole." Each day, place an object on the table that is made up of several pieces: i.e. a thermos, a coffee maker, a set of hot rollers, a tool kit, a box of stationery, a picnic basket equipped with plates and utensils. Separate the pieces and let students experiment with them. Ultimately, students may reassemble the gadgets!

*Note: Detailed diagrams may be inappropriate in some cases. Charts that typically show a child's body and skeletal system would suffice for this activity.

Link to Science
Contact local agencies like the American Heart Association, the American Lung Association and the American Red Cross. Frequently these organizations have educational materials available at a very reasonable price or free for the asking. Supplement your discussions about the parts of the body with this worthwhile information!

58. Mix and Match 'Em

There's some confusion among the animals!

Outcome
Students will make a whole, new animal from parts of various other animals.

Materials
- large animal stickers, magazine pictures of animals or animal rubber stamps
- construction paper
- scissors
- glue
- colored markers

Teacher Prep
Other than obtaining materials, the teacher should make a sample of the project so students will have a better understanding of what to do.

Group Activity
Discuss with students all of the places we can find animals. Pet stores and zoos may be common responses. On the chalk or marker board, list the animals found in such places: zebra, elephant, orangutan, lion, tiger, walrus, dog, cat, bird, fish, etc. From there, discuss the "parts" these animals have: tail, legs, hooves, tusks, snout, scales, hair and feathers. Have students imagine a dog with scales and tusks or a fish with legs!

Share your sample project with the class. Ask for student volunteers to name the parts which make up this imaginary animal. Explain that each student will mix and match animal parts to create a new, exotic animal. This can be done in a variety of ways:

1. Provide magazine pictures of animals. Students can cut out pieces of the animals and share that which isn't being used. The animals can be assembled on construction paper with glue.

2. Medium to large animal stickers can be cut up and assembled with different animal parts quite easily.

3. There are some rubber stamp kits available which allow children to create imaginary animals by mixing and matching heads, bodies and legs.

4. Playskool™ Animal Match-Ups™ for ages 2 and up allow children to create lots of different animals from 24 snap-together pieces.

Link to Language
Set up a display area in your classroom. Title it "Mixed-Up Animals." Students should give their animals names based upon the ones used. For example, "zelephant" might be the name for a combination zebra/elephant!

59. Parts of a Flower

This is the perfect math/science activity for all of your nature enthusiasts!

Outcome

Students will be introduced to the idea that parts together create a whole as they examine the parts of a flower.

Materials

- flower for each student
- piece of construction paper for each student
- clear, adhesive tape
- carrot with stem intact
- small bowl of water

To the Teacher

This science activity has a mathematical foundation: parts and whole. We discover the importance of parts: Each one has a special job which is necessary to the full functioning of the whole. The flower is a real-life example of this idea.

Teacher Prep

No preparation required other than obtaining materials.

Group Activity

Pair off students, distribute flowers and encourage the teams to discuss what they can observe about their flowers. Conversations may start with color, size and texture. We call these *attributes*. Upon closer examination, students may discuss the number of petals or leaves the flowers have.

Ask student volunteers to name the individual parts of the flower. The complexity of the responses will vary among students. Acceptable answers should include petals, stem, leaves, roots and seeds.

After the discussion, have students fold their papers in half lengthwise. On the left half, students can draw pictures depicting the live flower. On the right half, students can dissect or take apart the actual flowers and identify the petals, stem and leaves. Demonstrate how each piece can be taped to the right side and labeled. If labeling the flower parts is too challenging, supply students with ready-made adhesive labels which say "petal," "stem" and "flower."

Pass around a carrot with its stem intact. Have students identify the "root." This is the orange, palatable part of the vegetable. Slice the carrot so that only the first, top ½" (1.27 cm) of the carrot remains. Trim the greenery and set the "carrot plant" in a bowl of water (just covering the root), in a sunny spot. Observe the changes that occur. Student volunteers can be called upon to answer such questions as:

1. Where is the stem?
2. Where are the leaves?
3. What happened to the plant several days after it was cut, trimmed, and placed in water?
4. Would this plant grow in the same way if it didn't have a stem, leaves, or roots?

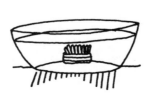

Link to Literature

The Tree: A First Discovery Book *by Gallimard Jeuneese and Pascale de Bourgoing (Scholastic Inc., 1989) has beautiful transparent overlays that show the life cycle of a chestnut tree. Trees are plants that have several parts, too. Find a tree outside and discuss the parts: a trunk, branches, roots, leaves and seeds. Sometimes you'll find trees that have blossoms, such as cherry and apple trees. Take a piece of white paper and brown crayon. Do a crayon rubbing of the tree bark for a memento!*

60. All Aboard the Ordinal Choo-Choo

Bring the excitement of railroads, engines and boxcars into your classroom as students create and display an ordinal train!

Outcome
Students will use ordinal numbers and will become familiar with the following terms: *engine, tender, boxcar* and *caboose*.

Materials

- reproducible train patterns (page 105)
- construction paper
- paper fasteners
- crayons, paint or markers
- scissors

Teacher Prep
Using the train patterns provided, reproduce and enlarge if necessary. Copy the patterns onto white card stock or construction paper. Several trains can be made and displayed, or one long train. Your decision will be based on the number of students in your class and the availability of display space.

Group Activity
Distribute the engine, tender, cars and caboose to students. If students are able to cut, have them cut out the various train pieces. If student cannot cut, the teacher can do this as part of the Teacher Prep.

Encourage students to decorate their train pieces using crayons, paint or markers. Students' names can be written on the back of each piece.

When the pieces are dry or ready to be assembled, use the paper fasteners. This also gives the effect of couplers (that which connects cars and locomotives). The order of the train should be the locomotive first, then the tender, boxcars and finally, the caboose. As the teacher assembles the train, make a note on paper as to which child's is first, second, third, etc. This will serve as the ordinal answer key.

The teacher can then ask students whose engine, tender, car or caboose is first, second, third, fourth, fifth . . . . Students will then respond. An alternative would be pointing to the piece and saying, "Danielle, this is your piece. Is it first, second, . . . ?"

One Step Further
Sequencing is also a readiness skill. Use the following terms to reinforce those skills: *first, second, next, then, finally.* Simple recipes also require sequencing. Choose a three- or four-step recipe and prepare it in class with your students. After reading it aloud and slowly, ask children to recall the ingredients and steps during the preparation.

Link to Literature
Freight Train by *Donald Crews (Puffin Books, Viking Penguin, 1985, Greenwillow Books. New York, 1978) is a Caldecott Honor Book which focuses on the journey of a very colorful train. This classic can be used to illustrate and supplement the terminology used in the group activity.*

61. Colored Cubes

Large or small it's fun for all!

Outcome
Students will recognize patterns in the arrangement of cubes.

Materials
- wooden cubes of various colors
- long sheet of white butcher paper

To the Teacher
This patterning activity can be done using several kinds of manipulatives. Plastic links, attribute blocks, pattern blocks, colored tiles or chips are some alternatives. The teacher may want to use a different manipulative each week to reinforce the same skills or to increase the difficulty. In this way boredom with tasks can be significantly reduced or even eliminated!

Teacher Prep
None required other than obtaining materials.

Group Activity
Lay the white butcher paper on the floor. Put colored cubes on the paper in a pile. Have five students select one cube each to put in a straight line on the paper. Select another student who repeats the five-cube pattern. The conversation might go like this:

Teacher: Bill, there are five cubes on the floor. What color is the first cube?

Bill: The first cube is green.

Teacher: Can you find another green cube in the pile and put it next to the fifth cube? What color is the second cube, Bill?

Bill: It is red.

Teacher: Can you find another red cube in the pile and put it next to the green cube you just picked?

Alternatively, a different student can be selected to continue each cube in the pattern.

One Step Further
Create a math center with any of the manipulatives suggested in To the Teacher or the Group Activity. Using large index cards, create patterns for each student to make with the manipulatives. To make the cards more difficult, leave out some of the information and put blank lines in their place.

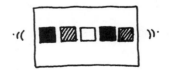

Link to Art
Using gift boxes or small cardboard boxes, create an extra-large set of colored cubes. Colored butcher paper or poster paint can be applied directly to the boxes. When dry, students can work cooperatively to make a large pattern across the classroom floor.

62. People Patterns

Lights! Camera! People in action!

Outcome
Students will use gross motor skills to form a live pattern.

Materials
- students
- camera with film
- cassette recorder and tape
- video camera and tape (optional)

Opening Activity
Review the concept of patterning with students before starting the group activity. This can be accomplished easily through the use of connecting cubes: red cube, white cube, blue cube, red, white, blue . . . .

Ask student volunteers to create more complicated patterns with the cubes in front of classmates. Repetition in design of organization is the key.

Teacher Prep
No preparation required.

Group Activity
Select three students to stand in front of the class. Standing one beside the other, each student will strike a different pose. For example, Kevin might raise both arms. Li-An might fold both arms. William might cross his left leg over his right one. Select three additional students to repeat this three-person pattern. Continue selecting students until everyone strikes a pose.

This activity can become as complex as the students can manage. Not only can hand/arm position and leg position vary, so can posture, facial expression and direction.

Some other ideas for people patterns are

1. First three people strike same pose, next three a different one, next three a different one and so on.

2. One student selects a standing pose, the next a sitting pose, the next a standing and so on.

3. One student faces the front standing, one faces the back standing, one faces the front sitting, one faces the back sitting and so on.

4. One student makes a barking sound, one a meow sound, one a clap; repeat.

Link to Language
This activity would make a dynamite presentation of the People Patterns. Tape-record voice patterns described in alternate activity 4. If you have access to a video camera, capture the experience on videotape. Best yet, have parents participate in a People Pattern at your school event!

63. Rush Hour

It's traffic time! Can you figure out which car is first, second or third in line?

Outcome

Students will become familiar with the concept of ordering. They will be able to place cars in a line ordinally and be able to identify the cars in the ordinal lineup.

Materials

• 10 die-cast cars of different colors
• highway mat or a highway drawing on poster board

Teacher Prep

The area on which this activity is played is a highway. Traffic is a familiar concept to children, especially if they live in a big city. Highway mats are commercially available and range in price. The mat and die-cast cars are popular toys outside of the math activity. One of the purposes of this task is to use materials that you may already have at your school. If you don't have or are unable to purchase a mat, improvise with a piece of poster board and a black marking pen.

Opening Activity

Start by calling students' names and having them line up behind you. As students are called, tell them the order in which they're lining up. For example: "Melissa, you are first. Ahmad, you are second. Justine, you are third . . . ."

In order, from the beginning of the line, ask each student what number he is in this line. If the task is too complicated, the students and teacher can count together. Reverse the order by starting at the end of the line and counting.

Group Activity

After collecting the die-cast cars, ask various students to select a particular car that you name and to put it on the highway first, second, third, fourth, fifth, . . . tenth.

When all of the cars have been arranged on the mat, ask a student to retrieve the fifth car. Replace the fifth car after it has been retrieved and ask another student to retrieve the eighth car. Replace it, and start again.

One Step Further

Create a more complicated game by having students switch the second and third cars or the first and tenth cars. Add more cars to the highway as students successfully complete the simpler tasks.

Link to Social Studies

Students will have lots of fun decorating a cardboard box to look like a car. Sketch commonly found car features (doors, windows, windshield wipers, trunk) on the four sides of the box, then paint. Name this dramatic play piece the cardboard car!

64. Patterning Party

Students can have a rewarding experience by "chipping" in and working together!

Outcome

Students will use cooperative skills in a game format to build on patterns started by other classmates.

Materials

- colored chips or counters: red, blue, yellow and white (an alternative is construction paper squares)
- desk or hand bell
- table space for each student

Teacher Prep

No preparation required other than obtaining materials.

Group Activity

Station students around the tables at which they will be working. Put several chips of each color in the center of each work table. When given the signal by the teacher, students individually start constructing a pattern with the chips in their own work space. Some examples of patterns students might construct appear below.

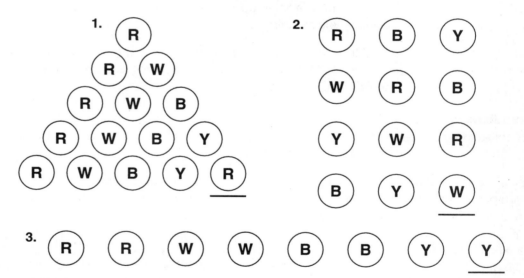

At the sound of the first bell, all students stop construction. At the sound of the second bell, students rotate in a clockwise or counterclockwise circle to the next student's work space and continue building on that student's pattern.

Repeat these steps after the majority of students have duplicated the pattern once. This activity can continue until all the chips have been used.

Encourage cooperative group work! If students have difficulty identifying the pattern or repeating it, suggest that "neighbors" help each other.

65. 1s, 2s, 5s & 10s

These patterns aren't perplexing but lots of fun!

Outcome
Students will search for patterns in numbers.

2, 4, 6, 8...

Materials
- 1 of the following: a 100s pocket chart, a transparency of a 100s chart, a poster 100s chart
- 4 1-100 charts per student
- crayon

5, 10, 15, 20...

Teacher Prep
Select your medium for this classroom activity. If you're using a pocket chart, you will need the corresponding number cards (1-100). If you're using a transparency chart, an overhead projector and overhead marking pens are necessary. If you're using a poster-quality chart, laminate it, and then use dry board marking pens so the chart can be reused. Duplicate a chart that is numbered from 1-100. There should be four copies per student.

Group Activity
As a group, count the numbers on the chart by ones. As students count, teacher and students can put an *X* through each number. Ask the class what they notice about the chart after the counting. The "pattern" is every number is crossed out.

The teacher prepares the chart-visual for the next exercise. Students will use their second clean chart. Count by 2s, crossing out each number that is increased by two. What is the pattern? Every other column is crossed out. Continue with the 5s and 10s. What are the patterns? For the 5s, every fifth column is crossed out. For the 10s, only the tenth column is crossed out.

One Step Further
Using an old magazine, fold every second, fifth or tenth page. Every page that is folded should be folded in the same way. Examine the pattern when the magazine is closed. What do your students observe? Experiment with other numbers: fold every third or fourth page. These activities cross over into Numbers and Counting, too!

Link to Language
Can you think of some games which rely upon the use of patterns? Some examples are various versions of bingo, checkers and chess! Challenge students to think of common items which contain some kind of pattern.

66. Letter Patterns

What do letters and math have in common? Patterns!

Outcome
Students will create patterns using letters of the alphabet.

Materials
- 1 of the following letter sets: press-out letters (available in educational supply stores), stenciled letters on construction paper or traceable letter patterns on construction paper
- pattern task cards made on 5" x 8" (12.7 x 20.32 cm) index cards

Teacher Prep
Prepare a set of letters using one of the suggestions from the Materials list. Several copies of each letter should be included. For young children, start with all capital letters. For older students, upper and lowercase letters can be mixed. You may also select different fonts, or letter styles, to be mixed within the set. Laminate the letters for prolonged classroom use. Letters can be stored in a plastic, see-through shoe box for easy identification. Teacher-made task cards can also be stored with the letter sets.

Group Activity
This is another ideal learning center for one or two students. As discussed earlier, patterning involves the repetition of a design or arrangement of objects. Students have unlimited ways of arranging letters into patterns:

1. A B A B A B A B – the repetition of two upper-case letters.

2. A Z A Z A Z A Z A Z – the repetition of using letters from alternating ends of the alphabet.

3. R s R s R s R s – the repetition of using upper-case, lowercase.

4. w W w W w W w W – the repetition of alternating fonts and sizes.

One Step Further
Create a symmetry activity by challenging students to create the mirror image of their patterns.

Links to Language and Art
Purchase a template that has the letters of the alphabet (the larger the better). Put the template, white paper and pencils with the "Letter Patterns" activity center. Students can practice creating letter patterns from stencils while practicing fine motor skills and letter formation!

67. Tools of the Trade

What do a bathroom scale, a watch and a meat thermometer have in common?

Outcome

Students will determine the best measuring tool to be used in specific situations.

Materials

- set of measuring cups and spoons
- analog clock, a digital clock, a watch
- bathroom scale, a food scale, a postage scale
- indoor/outdoor thermometer, a meat thermometer, an oral thermometer
- ruler and a tape measure
- 1-year calendar
- butcher paper and marking pen

Teacher Prep

Plan this activity over a series of days. Each day, three or four measuring devices can be introduced to the class. Responses can be recorded on a classroom chart made from butcher paper.

For example, the response chart might have the labels "measuring cups," "postage scale" and "tape measure" written across the top. Vertical labels might be: the weight of a letter, the amount of milk needed for a recipe and the dimensions of a door. Student volunteers can mark the appropriate boxes which correctly match the devices to the objects.

Group Activity

Facilitate a class discussion about measurement. Questions for thought would include:

1. What are some things that help us measure?
2. What objects can be measured using a ruler?
3. What can a scale tell us?
4. What can a watch tell us?

Introduce students to the butcher paper chart. Tell them over the next few days, they will decide upon the best tools for measuring certain items. For a *very* visual and hands-on experience, have the measuring devices and objects available before the lesson starts.

Using the example in Teacher Prep, place a set of measuring cups, postage scale, tape measure, a letter and a container of milk on the table. Students, with teacher help if necessary, identify each of the measuring tools. Ask students to match the letter with one of the tools. Students can then demonstrate how to measure a letter. Repeat this process with the container of milk and the classroom door. Document the results on the response chart. The next day students might investigate an oral thermometer, a one-year calendar and an analog clock!

Link to Science

Many science activities require some sort of measuring. One simple way to make the math/science connection is to graph daily outdoor temperatures. Older students can calculate the average daily temperature over a one-month period. This extension utilizes two common measuring tools: the thermometer and calendar!

68. I Can Measure

You don't need a ruler to measure things! This activity emphasizes the use of alternative units to illustrate the meaning of measurement.

Outcome

Students will determine length and width of objects in the classroom using nonstandard units of measure.

Materials

- large, plastic-coated paper clips (large, plastic links may be substituted for very young children)
- chalkboard or marker board eraser
- plastic straws
- chart to compare results
- several objects from the classroom

Teacher Prep

Link several paper clips together for each student. Provide several small objects which can easily be measured with the paper clips. Items may include a dish from the housekeeping center, a picture book and a paintbrush.

Group Activity

Demonstrate for students how they can measure an object, such as a book, by lining up the edge of the book with the edge of the first paper clip. Count to see how many paper clips it took to cover the length of the book. Repeat the experience using other objects. Allow students to practice together in small groups.

Once students have mastered measuring with paper clips, try using other nonstandard units of measure such as erasers and straws. Compare the results on a classroom chart. Ask students which device would be easier to use when measuring the floor, paper clips or straws? Why? Then, as a class project, measure the floor using all three devices: paper clips, straws and erasers.

One Step Further

This also makes a terrific activity center for children. Provide several objects to be measured and paper clips or plastic links. Have students sort items into two groups: long and short.

Link to Science

Measure the height of each student in your class. Create a special growth chart and record students' height every month. Make predictions about how many inches or centimeters the class altogether will grow in the course of a school year.

69. What's My Length?

There are lots of ways to measure things! Beads on a string are one fun way.

Outcome
Students will string beads on lanyard and will measure objects using the string of beads.

Materials
- plastic or wooden beads (available at craft stores)
- 1 piece of lanyard per student (length is at the teacher's discretion)
- several objects which can be measured in terms of length
- class chart to document length of objects

Teacher Prep
Shop around for beads and lanyard. They can usually be purchased at craft or hobby stores. Beads come in a variety of sizes, styles and colors. Many beads are made of plastic. Another alternative is wooden beads, though the price for these may be more than the plastic beads.

If you are doing a lesson on colors, for example, purple, then you can simply purchase all purple beads. The stringing of the beads can also become a patterning and sequencing activity if you use more than one color. It's important to note that the beads should have a wide enough opening so students can string them with ease.

Lanyard is a type of flexible, plastic string that also varies in color. Lanyard is typically used for craft purposes. Depending on the size of the beads, you may cut pieces of lanyard from six to twelve inches. Put a knot in one end of each student's piece before students start to string the beads.

Group Activity
You will need to designate how many beads are allotted to each student. The size of the beads should all be the same, as well as the number of beads each student gets. As each student completes the stringing of the beads, put a knot in the other end of the lanyard. By tying off both ends, you prevent beads from slipping off the string.

Provide several items for students to measure using their string of beads. Demonstrate how objects should be measured: line up the end of the first bead with the end of the object. All of the beads should be side by side when measuring. Compare the beads that line up with the object. The students should be able to say "The book is 7 beads long" or something similar to that.

Record students' measurements of each object on a chart and compare answers. You may even have some students demonstrate for the class how they measured certain objects.

Link to Science
Planting projects are always lots of fun. Bean seeds are well known for their quick sprouting. After planting seeds, have students measure their growth using the string of beads. Chart the growth of your plants. For an added challenge, grow different kinds of seeds and compare their growth. Which grows faster?

70. Much to Be Said About a Foot

Everyone has a chance to participate, even the parents!

Outcome
Students will estimate length and width of objects. They will learn to line up the edge of a ruler with the edge of an object, and they will measure objects with a foot-ruler.

Materials
- foot-ruler for each student (see Teacher Prep)
- several objects for students to measure (see Group Activity)
- record sheet

Teacher Prep
To create a foot-ruler, take a piece of lightweight cardboard or construction paper and cut it into several pieces, the dimensions of which should be 1" x 12." Laminate for durability. No lines (to indicate fractions of an inch) or numerals (to indicate full inches) are necessary. This instrument represents 12 inches or one foot. All measuring for the Group Activity will be done in feet.

Group Activity
Demonstrate for students how to measure by lining up a ruler with an object, such as a book. Emphasize the need to line up edges. If the book is one foot-ruler long and a little bit of a second foot-ruler, then consider the book one foot-ruler long. If the book is almost two foot-rulers long, then two would be a better choice for an answer.

Distribute the foot-rulers and ask each student to demonstrate this task. Once students understand how to measure an object, divide them into small groups. The groups will then report to their tables to measure the objects before them. Each student should have at least one object to measure. A simple chart can be left at each table for students to document their results.

Object	Foot-Rulers
Book	1
Table	4
Shoe	1
Door	6

One Step Further
If students require a greater challenge, have them estimate length and width to the nearest six inches (one-half of a foot-ruler). For example, a table might be 3½ foot-rulers long or 3½ feet. If the table were more than 3½ foot-rulers, round the answer to 4 feet.

Link to Language
Have each student illustrate one of the objects used in this measuring activity on a piece of white construction paper. As they dictate the length or width of the objects in foot-stick terms, the teacher can copy what is dictated below the pictures. Assemble this class book and make a large, butcher paper envelope in which the book can be kept. Send the book home each afternoon with a different student. Include a letter for parents which describes the activity and the results. Don't forget a piece of paper attached to the envelope for parent responses!

71. My Paper Doll

How tall are you? Make a paper model and find out!

Outcome

Each student will make a life-size paper doll of herself and will measure the paper doll to determine her height.

Materials

- white butcher paper
- crayons or colored markers
- scissors
- 12" rulers
- index cards

Teacher Prep

Obtain materials and cut butcher paper to the approximate size of each child. Model how you expect students to complete the task.

1. After cutting a sheet of butcher paper, ask a student to volunteer to lay down (backside) on the paper.

2. Take a crayon and trace around the student's figure.

3. After each student has traced the other, they cut around their own paper dolls.

4. Decide whether students should measure in inches or feet, and show them how to measure the paper doll from head to toes. Students should round their measurement to the closest foot or inch.

5. Record the height and "label" (inches or feet) on an index card; then tape it to the paper doll's head.

Group Activity

After the demonstration, pair students off and have each student go through the process of creating a life-size image of himself. Supervise students as they measure their paper dolls. Depending on student ability, it may be necessary for the teacher to assist in the measuring and recording.

One Step Further

For students who understand the idea of both feet and inches, have them measure the paper dolls with greater accuracy by recording their height in feet and inches. (For example: instead of just 3 feet or 36 inches, a closer measurement might be 3 feet, 5 inches.)

Links to Language and Art

Provide students with collage materials, fabric remnants, wallpaper books, markers and paint. Encourage students to decorate their paper dolls. Yarn can be used for hair, and don't forget the wonderful wiggly eyes (available in craft stores).

Have students record an "All About Me" message on a cassette tape. Questions students can answer include What's your favorite color? Where do you live? What are the names of the people in your family? What is your favorite thing to do?

72. Graphing Temperature

Will it be hot? How 'bout snow? How will anybody know?

Outcome
Students will observe changes in temperature over one week. They will record temperatures on a line graph and draw conclusions from the data.

Materials
- white butcher paper
- colored marking pens
- indoor/outdoor thermometer
- ruler

Teacher Prep
Prepare a butcher paper graph similar to the one in the margin. In creating a line graph, students must plot points and connect them with a ruler. Observations are made based upon the direction of the lines. If students are unable to read a thermometer, plot points or connect them, the teacher can do this and lead students through a series of questions pertaining to what they see on the graph.

Group Activity
Lead a class discussion on tools that help us measure. Rulers, tape measures, measuring cups and spoons, and scales are frequent replies. If the subject doesn't come up, ask students what a thermometer measures. A thermometer measures temperature: refrigerator or freezer temperatures food temperature, indoor and outdoor temperature, and body temperature. If at all possible, try obtaining the various kinds of thermometers previously mentioned. Are there differences or similarities between these tools?

Briefly demonstrate how thermometers are read. Mercury (the "red stuff") rising indicates a higher temperature. Thermometers measure temperature in terms of Fahrenheit or Celsius (metric, preferred over centigrade). The calibrations may be too small for some children to read, in which case the teacher can announce the temperature for each day. The measurement should be taken at the same time each day. After five days, what can your students say about the temperature outdoors?

Conduct this experiment over a two-week period. Does this change the five-day conclusion? Try the same experiment indoors. Don't forget to plot the data on the butcher paper line graph. Compare the indoor and outdoor results.

Link to Science
Tie in this activity with a unit on weather. There are several children's books available on this topic, for a variety of reading and interest levels. Weather myths, types of clouds, the water cycle, thunder and lightning are subjects students really enjoy.

Link to Literature
***The Cloud Book** by Tomie de Paola is a delightful book which would compliment your temperature and weather studies. The illustrations are large and bright. De Paola describes the ten types of cloud formations in a concise, nonthreatening language!*

73. Personal Growth Chart

The sky is definitely the limit with this measuring activity!

Outcome

Students will chart their growth monthly over a ten-month period of time. They will then make conclusions based upon the growth data.

Materials

- tape measure (such as one used for sewing)
- "incentive"-type chart used to record the growth of each student
- pencil

Teacher Prep

Attach the measuring tape to the wall using a staple gun. The low-number end should be perpendicular to the floor. Fill in the class chart with the name of each student. Across the top, record the day of each month that growth is measured. Mount the chart near the measuring tape. Decorate this special area with monthly or seasonal pictures, poems and/or photographs of students.

Group Activity

Designate one day of each month as a Growth Chart Day. Students should remove shoes before the measuring. Record data on the class chart. Include yourself (the teacher) in the activity. Conduct a group discussion as the monthly results are accumulated. Questions to ask the students: How many inches (or fractions of an inch) did you grow in one month? In two months? How many inches did the entire class grow from September to October?

For a very visual presentation, use calculator paper to show how many inches the group grows each month. Display the homemade tape measure at eye level for students to study. Add more inches to the calculator tape each month. Students can see how individual contributions are vital to the group!

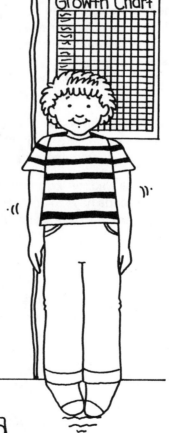

Link to Language

Students can reflect upon the idea of growth when writing their own acrostic poem.

Growth
Rapid
Ongoing
Wonderful
Towering
Height

74. Measuring Cup Madness

Bubble, bubble = No toil or trouble . . . .

Outcome
Students will determine the volume of measuring cups through experimentation.

Materials
- full set of measuring cups
  (alternatively, nesting cups can be used)
- sand
- water
- beans
- other items that can be measured

Teacher Prep and Group Activity
Allow students sufficient time to experiment with measuring cups. Measuring activities lend themselves nicely to a classroom math center.

The acquisition of several sets of measuring cups will allow many students to participate at one time. Plastic shoe boxes or small plastic totes are ideal containers to hold silicon sand (very fine, clean and used in most sandboxes), water colored with drops of food coloring, lima beans, pinto beans, rice and cotton are some suggested items that can be used at the measuring center. Each item should have its own container. Emphasize to students the importance of *not mixing* the items. This would have serious implications in the true value of their results.

A collection of empty containers which vary in size and depth would also compliment this measuring center. Students will discover through experimentation how many "scoops" of rice from the ½-cup device will fill the small plastic bowl or teacup.

Students will also realize the relationship the measuring cups have to one another: 2 scoops of beans from the ½ cup fit into the 1 cup, 4 scoops of sand from the ¼ cup fit into the 1 cup, etc.

Gradually add more equipment to the measuring center. This will help in eliminating boredom. Some examples are measuring spoons, measuring devices with metric calibrations, graduated beakers and measuring devices of differing shapes (i.e. square cups).

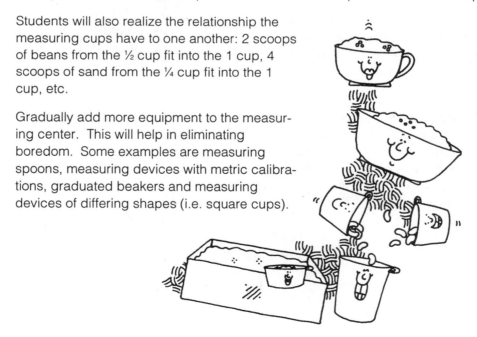

Link to Science
Let students put math into action by preparing a fun recipe! This extension activity demonstrates the important applications of measuring. Experiment by "mismeasuring" one ingredient and testing the results. For an extra challenge, double the recipe!

75. Lots of Area to Cover

Figuring surface area is a cinch with colored tiles your students can make!

Outcome
Students will create patterns to match a specific surface area.

Materials
- graph paper reproducible (page 106)
- set of colored tiles
- package of index cards
- colored markers
- resealable, plastic sandwich bags

Teacher Prep
In this open-ended activity students will use colored tiles to make patterns. These tiles are available through various companies which produce math manipulatives.

An inexpensive alternative is to make two copies of the graph paper reproducible. One copy should be made on construction paper or card stock, for a heavier manipulative. Students can color and cut the "tiles" out for use with this activity.

The second copy will be used as a type of measuring surface with the colored tiles. Each square on the graphing paper represents one cubic unit.

Create a set of task cards using blank, 3" x 5" (7.62 x 12.7 cm) index cards. Each card should have a number and the label "cubic unit(s)."

Group Activity
Each student should have a cubic unit sheet (the graph paper reproducible) and a set of colored tiles. As the teacher shows the class a number (such as 21 cubic units), students place 21 tiles on the graphing paper. There is a great degree of freedom in student responses. The only "rule" is that each tile must touch the complete side of another tile (see illustration). When the final task has been given to the class, students can document the experience by coloring the corresponding squares on the graph paper. Store the individual sets of colored tiles in resealable, plastic sandwich bags for use at another time.

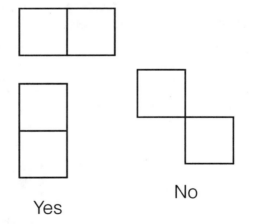

Yes

No

Link to Math
Use colored tiles to measure objects in the classroom or around the school. For example, how many colored tiles does is take to fill in the front cover of a book? Once students determine the number of tiles, answers are then labeled cubic units.

76. Our Day

What are we doing next? The question will always be answered with this special display.

Outcome
Students will associate classroom activities with a time schedule.

Materials
- small paper plates
- sentence strips
- clock face and hands reproducible (bottom of page)
- scissors for students
- paste or glue
- black marking pen
- paper fasteners
- photographs of various classroom activities

To the Teacher
Students frequently ask, "What are we going to do now?" Turn the question into a learning opportunity. After the display is assembled, encourage students to locate the next activity on the wall or bulletin board. Find the time next to it and compare the results with the analog or digital clock available in the classroom.

Teacher Prep
Take photographs of students at each activity that you plan for: line up, outdoor play, snack time, art, music, language, lunch time, nap time, etc. Under each photograph write the word or words that describe the activity. Enlarge and duplicate the clock face and hands below onto construction paper or card stock. After students assemble clocks, place them next to each picture which indicates when the activity begins and ends. Cut sentence strips into thirds and record the analog times as well.

Group Activity
Students cut out and paste the clock face reproducible and clock hands to the small paper plate. With teacher assistance, attach the clock hands with a paper fastener. Move hands into position and display.

Link to Science
Clocks are an example of a simple machine. The gears within the clock are toothed wheels. Ask a local watch or clock repairman to demonstrate for the class how this machine works. Obtain other simple machines which operate through the use of gears, such as a hand drill or eggbeater. Display them on a science table for students to examine.

Enlarge and duplicate

77. Special Days: A Time Line

Record birthdays, holidays, special class projects or theme days using the time line method.

Outcome
Students will learn sequence of events as they relate to time.

Materials

- calculator tape
- colored markers
- small photographs of students
- stickers representing holidays and special events
- 12 small banners representing each month of the year

To the Teacher
Time can be a difficult concept for children to understand. By linking time to a child's real-life experiences, the teacher helps create meaning. The two components of time are duration (how long) and sequence (what comes next).

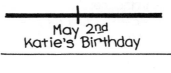

Teacher Prep
There is little initial preparation required. Daily maintenance will be the most important task. The time line can be displayed on a bulletin board or wall but should be at eye level to the students. Leave room above the time line for monthly banners. Start with the month in which your school year begins (such as September). Record in order birthdays, holidays and other special events which will take place in that month. Add blank tape as you get closer to the end of the piece with which you are working.

Group Activity
At daily circle or morning time, discuss with students the activities planned for the day. Perhaps there is a birthday, a student lost his first tooth or this week is Color Week. Document these important dates on the time line using photographs of students, stickers and marking pens. The time line is also a tool for reinforcing sequence of events. For older students, ask questions which require them to locate answers on the time line.

Extend this activity at home! Send a note home with students explaining the time line project done in class. For "homework," ask students and parents to write down one important date (include the year) and event which might be considered unusual: a family trip, a special occasion or a "first" (first bicycle, first allowance, etc.). The following day when students come to class, discuss the events and put them in order of occurrence. Document them on a new time line.

Link to Literature
As an introduction to time and sequencing, read Leo Lionni's book **A Busy Year** *(Scholastic: New York, 1992) to students. Follow two mice through the months of the year and the seasons as they make a friend named Woody, a charming talking tree!*

78. Morning, Afternoon or Evening?

Play the time game. When do you eat dinner? When does the sun rise?

Outcome
Students will identify activities as those done in the morning, afternoon, or evening.

Materials
- construction paper squares
- bag (brown bag, gift bag, etc.)
- colored markers
- reproducible signs, one each *morning, afternoon* and *evening* at bottom of page
- butcher paper or poster board

Teacher Prep
Enlarge, reproduce, color and laminate the morning, afternoon and evening signs below. Mount signs on butcher paper or poster board. On the construction paper squares, cut and paste pictures from magazines which represent a variety of activities: waking up, eating breakfast, nap time, eating dinner, playing outside, etc. Under each picture, provide a one- or two-word description of the activity. Laminate these symbol cards, cut apart and place them in a paper bag or a gift bag.

Group Activity
Allow each student to pull one of the cards from the bag. Ask the student if this activity is done in the morning, afternoon or evening. Encourage the student to explain why. Tape the card to the prepared chart made from butcher paper. This is an open-ended activity! Many activities can be done at a variety of times. If a student says she takes a nap in the morning (as opposed to afternoon) it is a possibility. Accept all answers that are justified by students.

Link to Social Studies
Send a letter home to parents which explains what you've been doing in class: studying morning, afternoon and evening. Ask parents to respond to these sentences: "Name something you do in the morning. Name something you do in the afternoon. Name something you do in the evening." Remind parents to return their answers to school the following day. Discuss the answers at circle time with the class. Add original responses to the morning, afternoon, evening chart.

Enlarge and duplicate

79. The Classroom Calendar

Make calendar time in your classroom extra special with a little help from your students.

Outcome
As students participate in calendar activities, they will observe sequencing of numbers (days) and understand the concept of day, month and year.

Materials
- blank calendar, preferably laminated (generic-type without name of month)
- construction paper squares to fit the days on the calendar (prenumbered according to the number of days in the month)
- colored pencils, markers and/or crayons

Group Activity
Give each student a construction paper square with a number on it. Encourage them to decorate their square for the classroom calendar. Discuss events that occur in that particular month. For example: October is in the fall with leaves turning many colors and includes Columbus Day, Halloween, student birthdays and Back-to-School Night. Students can use some of these ideas in their illustrations. On the back of each finished square, write the name of the student who did the artwork. On that day of the month, have the student who decorated the square place it on the calendar.

Additional Hints
Teachers can enhance the calendar lesson by asking such questions as:

- What day is it? (Mon., Tues., Wed., Thurs., Fri., Sat., Sun.)
- What month is it?
- What is the date? (1, 22, 30, 31, etc.)
- What is the year?
- What was yesterday?
- What was the date yesterday?
- What day will it be tomorrow?
- What will be the date tomorrow?

Link to Literature
Today Is Monday by Eric Carle (Scholastic: New York, 1993) can be used in conjunction with this activity or "Coming to Lunch?" (page 4) Carle uses the days of the week and fun-to-pronounce foods in a way that has high appeal for the teacher and student. His unique collage style, fun and repetitive vocabulary make this a book you'll want to read more than one time.

The simple text makes this piece of literature perfect for chorale readings. Students can be assigned to say certain sentences when given a cue. Other reading activities include the writing of each sentence on a sentence strip and displaying the strips in the classroom pocket chart. Use pictures in place of nouns on the sentence strips. Have the class rehearse the sentences each day for a week. Finally, serve each of the foods mentioned on the particular day of the week.

80. Shop 'Til You Drop!

Turn your dramatic play center into a clothing, stationery or grocery store.

Outcome
Students will participate in the roles of consumer and merchant. They will use play money to make purchases.

Materials
- designated area in the classroom for "the store"
- toy cash register or cash box
- play money
- for a grocery store: empty food containers such as cereal boxes, plastic gallon milk jugs, soda cans, cookie and cracker boxes
- for a clothing store: dress-up items such as dresses, overalls, hats, shoes and accessories
- for a stationery store: paper goods such as envelopes, pads of paper, paper clips, pencils, crayons, notebooks and scissors

Teacher Prep
After selecting the area in your classroom to serve as your store, set up suggested materials on a table. If you have ideas for other "stock items," feel free to add them to your store! Each item should be clearly marked with a price. This can be done by using folded index cards and a thick marking pen. Obtain a toy cash register, cash box or a sorting tray to separate play money. Other props you may choose to add to this area are brown bags, a special smock for the merchant to wear and baskets for shoppers.

Group Activity
Ask students what they buy when they go shopping. Some common answers are food, clothes, toys and books. Discuss the different kinds of stores and what each one sells. For example, a grocery store sells vegetables, fruits, meat, milk products, breads and cereals, frozen foods and other related items. A clothing store sells pants, shirts, shoes, undergarments, skirts, dresses and coats. Department stores sell a variety of things. Discuss the concept behind this kind of store: There are different departments or sections where many different things are sold, all under the same roof! There are many other kinds of stores or shops: gardening center, meat shop, jewelry store, bookstore, music shop and so on. Use some of these ideas to create a different dramatic play center each week!

Link to Literature
Alexander, Who Used to Be Rich Last Sunday *by Judith Viorst (Alladin, 1978) would compliment this shopping theme nicely! Discuss with students how they might spend a dollar. For older elementary students, try* ***The $1.00 Word Riddle Book*** *by Marilyn Burns.*

81. Time It—Graph It

Let's hop to it! How many times can you do . . . in one minute?

Outcome
Students will use large motor skills to accomplish timed tasks. They will see a relationship between activities and time and will compare results on a graph.

Materials

- outdoor toys such as a jump rope, ball, hoops, etc.
- timer or stopwatch
- butcher paper
- marking pen

Teacher Prep
Decide upon the tasks students will attempt in one minute. They might include jumping on two feet, hopping on one foot, swinging a hoop around the waist, jumping rope, filling and emptying buckets of sand and bouncing a ball. Prepare a large graph on butcher paper with the headings for the selected tasks.

Group Activity
Each day, select one task that each student will attempt in one minute and record the individual results on the graph. Take photographs of students as they participate in the various tasks for a snappy-looking bulletin board. Describe the activity represented in each group of pictures using one or two action words such as *hopping, running, jumping high* (or far) and *ball bouncing*. Not only will your children be learning math concepts but language skills, too! When the graph has been completed, discuss the findings. Ask students questions such as: Did it seem like you were . . . (jumping, hopping, etc.) for a long time? How many other students hopped the same number of times in each minute? How many minutes did everyone jump all together? How many times did everyone bounce the ball all together?

Link to Language
Create a class book titled **In One Minute, I Can . . .** Students finish the sentence and illustrate what they did. For example: "In one minute, I can jump rope 30 times." Send the book home each afternoon with a different child. A brief note explaining the activity and when to return the book should accompany the class publication.

82. Let's Make Money!

Turn your classroom into the U.S. Mint. Give students the opportunity to create their own classroom currency.

Outcome
Students will design their own currency and give value to the new currency.

Materials
- white, unlined paper (such as cotton bond or duplicating paper)
- pencils
- markers, colored pencils and/or crayons
- access to duplicating machine (optional: laminating machine)
- several *real* coins and bills

To the Teacher
Money is a fun manipulative. Children at a very young age understand that money is a valuable device which allows people to purchase items they need and want. Empower students by giving them the opportunity to design currency and give it value. For example, Luis might design a dollar bill with his face on it instead of George Washington's.

Teacher Prep
Collect a variety of coins and bills for the students to examine. Try to obtain currency from other countries as well. Set out drawing materials and currency on work tables.

Opening Activity
Introduce the different types of coins and bills to the students. Discuss the differences and similarities between the currency, such as color, size, weight, shape and value. Compare two items at a time and record results on a Venn diagram.

Group Activity
Direct students to the tables where the materials are set up. Explain to them it is "their turn" to create money. Things to consider would include characteristics discussed in the Opening Activity. After students have designed their money in pencil, duplicate several sheets of each student's innovation. Students can then color their money and cut out the pieces. For durability, the teacher can laminate the currency.

One Step Further
As a class, discuss and design classroom coins, laminate and use as incentives to "purchase" free time activities, extended recess or lunch with the teacher!

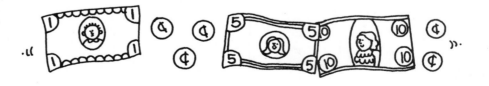

Link to Parents
Money Doesn't Grow on Trees: A Parent's Guide to Raising Financially Responsible Children *by Neale S. Godfrey and Carolina Edwards (A Fireside Book published by Simon & Schuster: New York, 1994.) is a marvelous resource for parents with children—young or old! Chapter titles include "How to Teach Your Child the Basics of Money Management" and "When to Start Your Children on an Allowance." For the very young, the authors have outlined several games parents can play with their children to introduce the concept of money.*

83. Coupon Collage

Grab the scissors and paste . . . . There's no time to waste!

Outcome

Students will use coupons as an alternative currency, sort coupons into food and non-food groups, and arrange coupons into a class collage.

Materials

- newspapers, magazines and supermarket advertisements containing coupons
- large sheet of white or colored butcher paper
- blunt scissors for students
- paste or glue

To the Teacher

Coupons are a form of money. Each manufacturer's coupon has a redeemable cash value, though usually very small. Coupons are great manipulatives for games and higher math problems. Locate some examples of coupons to share with students as a circle time activity or group activity.

Opening Activity

Show the students some examples of coupons. Ask students what they see on the coupon. Some responses might include a picture of the specific item, the "cents-off" value, description of the item, instructions to the consumer and clerk, an expiration date and a bar code. From a group of previously collected coupons, ask students to determine whether the coupons are for a food item or a nonfood item.

Group Activity

Allow students to work together and sort coupons into food and nonfood categories. Divide a large piece of butcher paper into two categories. Encourage students to paste the food coupons onto the food section of the butcher paper and the nonfood coupons onto the nonfood section.

One Step Further

Ask students to add various coupons and determine how much money can be saved. Introduce the idea of "double coupons" and have students figure out the value of a coupon if the amount is doubled.

Link to Technology

Take a field trip to a grocery store and watch how coupons are scanned. Bar codes on coupons make check-out time easier as the computer reads the bar code.

84. Make a Menu

Create a menu of healthy snacks, lunch-time munchables or favorite desserts.

Outcome
Students will create a list of food items and assign a price to each item.

Materials
- 9" x 12" (22.86 x 30.48 cm) sheet of construction paper for each student
- pencils
- markers, colored pencils and/or crayons
- ruler or straight edge
- children's menus from restaurants
- play money

Teacher Prep
There are many things on menus which relate to math concepts: categories and prices are the most obvious. Using the overhead projector or chalkboard, write some of the menu items with the prices down for all students to see at once. Set out the suggested materials on the work table.

Opening Activity
Assemble students into a circle for a circle time discussion about menus. Ask students to name their favorite foods and where they like to eat. Distribute the menus and allow students to work in groups. Students can share menu favorites with other group members. Discuss prices of menu items.

To the Teacher
It would be easier for students to grasp the idea of cost if menu prices were rounded to the nearest dollar or quarter. This would vary according to the ability of your students. Use play money to illustrate the prices.

Link to Art
Jazz up menus with stencils, pictures cut from magazines, and stickers. Create a menu theme, such as desserts, and decorate a classroom bulletin board titled "Sweet Treats."

85. Money Bingo

Your best bet in learning how to have fun with money!

Outcome
Students will identify amounts of money under $1.00.

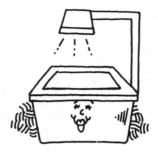

Materials
- copy of the Money Bingo reproducible for each student (page 104)
- crayon
- overhead projector
- set of overhead coins (optional: overhead bills)

To the Teacher
Learning to use money is a life-skill we are faced with every day. Introduce the topic by asking children what people do with money. Discuss the kinds of things people buy with money, such as food, clothing cars, books, toys and services (i.e. a gardener's services and a doctor's services). Review the value of commonly used coins: a penny equals one cent, a nickel equals five cents, a dime equals ten cents and a quarter equals twenty-five cents.

Teacher Prep
Prepare bingo cards by first making several copies of the Money Bingo sheet. Randomly place amounts of money in each box. After creating five or six master bingo sheets, reproduce an ample number of sheets for your entire class.

Opening Activity
Practice making sets of coins and counting the value. Students can work in pairs where one student creates a set of coins, and the other counts the amount. Students then switch roles and continue the game.

Group Activity
It's bingo time! Each student has one bingo sheet (see Teacher Prep) and a crayon. The teacher randomly creates sets using overhead coins on the overhead projector. As students see the projected coins, they determine the amount and look for it on their bingo sheets. Students put an *X* on the square if the amount in the square matches the one that is projected. Encourage students to help each other if assistance is needed. The first ones to get five *X*s in a row horizontally, vertically or diagonally are the winners.

One Step Further
Create a more complicated Money Bingo game by increasing the amounts of money displayed on the bingo sheet. This could include the use of overhead bills and less commonly used coins such as the fifty-cent piece. Let students take turns leading the bingo game and placing overhead money on the projector.

Link to Social Studies
Obtain a variety of foreign coins and bills from a local foreign exchange broker (check your Yellow Pages directory). Show students the exchange value of the foreign currency with U.S. currency. Teach students the names of foreign currency such as francs (France), lira (Italy and Turkey) and pound (United Kingdom and various other countries).

86. Shopping Bag Switch

Everybody loves to shop, and these bags are already filled.

Outcome
Students will calculate the cost of selected items in shopping bags.

Materials
- toy grocery items: fruit, vegetables, bottles of milk or soda, eggs, bread, cereal, hot dogs, etc.
- grooming items: brushes, combs, curlers, barrettes, hair ribbons, toothbrush, bar of soap, etc.
- stationery items: pads of paper, envelopes, pencils, pens, crayons, erasers, telephone book, etc.
- adhesive tape

- athletic items: baseball, bat, football, soccer ball, basketball, golf club and ball, etc.
- toy store items: cars, trucks, dolls, games, modeling clay, puzzles, plastic dinosaurs, etc.
- several large brown bags
- package of large price tags
- marking pen

Teacher Prep
Collect the suggested materials. Determine a price for each item. Write the price on a tag and tape it to the object. Do this for every object. Each set of materials will go into a separate brown bag. For example, cars, trucks, dolls, games, modeling clay, puzzles and plastic dinosaurs would all go into a brown bag labeled "Toy Store Items." Feel free to make up other theme bags such as art supplies, aquarium supplies or bookstore items.

Group Activity
Divide the class into small groups. Ask for a representative from each group to come forward and select a theme bag. When each group has a bag, set them loose to complete the following tasks:

1. Put the items in order from least expensive to the most expensive (concept: ordering).

2. Be prepared to name the least expensive item and most expensive item (concept: comparing).

3. What is the total cost of the items? (concept: whole number operations)

4. Would there be any change left over if you paid with a $5 bill?

5. What is the range in price? Subtract the lowest price from the highest price (concept: statistics).

6. **Super Challenge!** What is the average cost of the items? The sum divided by the quantity of numbers (concept: statistics).

When the groups have answered the questions pertaining to the first bag, have them switch bags and start all over!

Links to Language and Art
Before putting items in their respective brown bags, have each group decorate a bag! Some fun suggestions: a collage of magazine pictures and words that best represents the contents, crayon resist (heavy crayon drawing covered by a watercolor wash) or 3-D effect (miniature cars, animals, books, etc., glued onto the outside of the bag.

87. Catalog Craze

Go shopping without ever leaving your classroom!

Outcome

Students will choose their favorite items from a catalog and will calculate the total cost of selected items.

Materials
- collection of toy catalogs (abundant during holiday times)
- paper and pencil
- calculator (optional)

To the Teacher

This activity is geared more toward the older primary student, however modifications can be made to accommodate any age of child. Give students plenty of time to peruse the catalogs. If carefully observed, you'll see how students can create their own math experiences from this inexpensive manipulative. Examples of higher level thinking skills include price comparisons of exact items from different catalog companies, making choices and budgeting. This activity also promotes positive social interaction between peers.

Teacher Prep

Start collecting toy catalogs well in advance of this activity. Send a letter home to parents explaining an upcoming math activity on money and the need for toy catalogs. Catalogs of this nature are popular during the holidays. They are also available through some department stores that provide mail order services.

Group Activity

Tell students this is their opportunity to create a wish list. Using the toy catalogs, paper and a pencil, list the items, quantity and price per unit of the toys he or she would like. Students then calculate the total. A calculator can be used in addition to or in place of paper and pencil.

One Step Further

Increase the difficulty of this task by asking students to figure shipping and handling charges with the subtotals. Sometimes companies charge a percentage of the subtotal or a flat rate (i.e. $2.50).

Stepping Back

Early primary students can total the purchases by only adding the whole numbers (those numbers to the left of the decimal point).

Link to Literature
The Kids' Money Book by Neale S. Godfrey (Scholastic, 1991) is a marvelous resource for children and adults! The question and answer format is very effective as are the numerous illustrations and photographs. The history of money, banking and credit are only some of the worthwhile topics addressed in this book.

88. Sammy the Sum-Muncher

Feed Sammy the answers to addition problems.

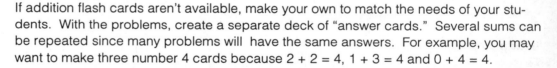

Outcome
Students will calculate answers to basic addition facts.

Materials
- paper lunch bag
- materials to decorate puppet: wiggly eyes, colored markers, yarn, glue, construction paper
- 2 small baskets or decorated boxes
- 2 signs, made from index cards: one with a smiling face, the other with the words *Try Again*
- 3" x 5" (7.62 x 12.7 cm) index cards or addition flash cards

Teacher Prep
Much of the preparation involves the creation of **Sammy the Sum-Muncher.** Start with a paper bag. Position the bag so the bottom side is up. When you place your hand in the upside-down paper bag, the "bottom" becomes the head of Sammy. A "mouth" is created where the crease appears. How you decorate Sammy is up to you. Sammy can be a boy or a girl (Samantha). Yarn can be used for hair, wiggly eyes can contribute to a humorous and more animated Sammy puppet. Don't forget a nose and, very important—a mouth! An outfit can easily be made from construction paper and glued to the rest of the paper bag.

If addition flash cards aren't available, make your own to match the needs of your students. With the problems, create a separate deck of "answer cards." Several sums can be repeated since many problems will have the same answers. For example, you may want to make three number 4 cards because 2 + 2 = 4, 1 + 3 = 4 and 0 + 4 = 4.

The two baskets or boxes should be labeled with the signs: a smiling face and "Try Again."

Group Activity
Assemble students in a circle on the floor. Introduce them to Sammy the Sum-Muncher. Lay answer cards faceup on the chalkboard tray or floor. As you show students the addition problems, ask individuals to locate the matching answer or sum card and put it in Sammy's mouth. Sammy (with a little help from the teacher) deposits the answer card in one of the two baskets. If the answer is correct, the teacher can reinforce the good work with positive verbal cues, or Sammy can award the student with a sticker. If the answer is incorrect, Sammy places the answer card in the Try Again basket. Students can then work with the individual to arrive at another answer.

One Step Further
Sammy can be used to reinforce other math, language and science concepts: subtraction and multiplication facts, number and shape recognition, letter and name identification, animal babies and mothers.

Links to Language and Art

With students so highly motivated at this point, why not let each student make a Sammy puppet or another puppet of his choice? Puppets made from paper bags are easy and inexpensive. Toilet paper tubes and construction paper make great characters, too. Allow students to create their own puppet show! Send the puppets home with a note that tells parents how you have been using the puppets in class.

89. Fact Pack

Students and parents will enjoy this refreshing approach to adding and subtracting.

Outcome
Students will practice addition and subtraction facts using manipulatives.

Materials

- brown construction paper
- brown felt-tipped marker
- paper punch-jumbo-sized
  bear (available in stationery,
  craft and educational supply stores)
- index cards
- resealable sandwich bags
- lamination
- parent note

To the Teacher
It's important for parents to know what their children are learning at school. It's even more important to involve parents whenever we can. This activity is two-fold. It's a way for students to practice math facts and a means of promoting parent involvement in the home setting. Parents as partners become one of your greatest assets! Whenever possible, involve them in the education process.

Teacher Prep
Paper punches become a valuable tool in the teacher's classroom. There are two sizes: small and jumbo (large). There are many shapes from which to choose, and they're an affordable investment. In this activity, the jumbo bear punch is suggested. If you don't have access to these kinds of punches, there are alternatives. Prepackaged, die-cut bear shapes (usually used for calendar days) are available in educational supply stores: bears can be made by teachers using the Ellison Letter Machine (usually found in teacher resource rooms), or bear patterns can be duplicated onto brown paper.

A math kit should be made for each student in your class. First, write a series of math facts on 5-10 index cards (one problem per card). Answers can be written on the back of each card.

Next, "punch" several bears from brown, laminated construction paper. Enough should be punched to solve the problem with the greatest sum. Likewise, enough should be punched for the largest number in a subtraction problem.

Finally, store the flash cards and manipulatives in a resealable sandwich bag for each student. Include a parent letter which explains how to use the Fact Pack with their child:

> Dear Parent:
> We are studying addition and subtraction facts. Enclosed are some facts we've been practicing at school. With the flash cards are bear counters, which you and your child can use in solving the problems. The activity only takes a few minutes. More important, it allows you and your child to work together in a fun way!
>
> Thanks,

Link to Literature
Brown Bear, Brown Bear, What Do You See? *by Bill Martin, Jr. and pictures by Eric Carle (New York: Holt, Rinehart and Winston, Inc., 1967) is a classic children's book that explores colors. Use this math activity and book as a springboard for a unit on bears! Using resources from the public library and bookstores, research the different kinds of bears, what they look like and where they live.*

90. Shoe Bag Frenzy

Addition is "in the bag" with this exciting activity center!

Outcome
Students will solve addition problems with the use of manipulatives.

Materials
- shoe bag
- various manipulatives
- small index cards
- colored markers
- self-adhesive labels

Teacher Prep
Shoe bags typically come with 12 pockets. Number the self-adhesive labels from 1-12. Place each label on the individual pockets. Within each pocket put a matching number of manipulatives. For example, a die-cast car can go into the pocket labeled "1," two pattern blocks can go into the pocket labeled "2," three keys can go into the pocket labeled "3" and so on.

On the index cards, write number sentences which students will solve: 3 + 4 = ?, 1 + 2 = ? The activity can be self-checking by writing the sum (the answer to an addition problem) on the back of each index card with a series of corresponding dots. Assemble the finished index cards into a deck with a rubber band.

Group Activity
One student selects a card from the deck. He or she goes to the corresponding pockets and pulls out the manipulatives. After counting all the objects, the student reveals the answer. If the answer is correct, the student separates the manipulatives and puts them back into the original pockets. Then the next student takes another card from the deck and repeats the activity steps. The difficulty can be increased by labeling the pockets with higher numbers.

This activity can be used as a center, which students visit individually or in pairs. It can also be used within a large or small group, where students solve the problems in front of the class.

One Step Further
Title the activity "Pockets Full of Money" and use toy coins and bills inside of each pocket. Create task cards that have pictures of the manipulatives instead of numbers. For example, die-cast car + keys = ? (1 + 3 = 4).

Link to Art
Using construction paper and a pencil, trace around students' shoes. After decorating one side, have students cut out the shoe patterns. Write number sentences on the back of the shoes, instead of writing addition problems on index cards. Laminate the "shoes" and store them in a shoe box next to the shoe bag activity!

91. What's the Problem?

The teacher has the solution, but can you name the problem?

Outcome
Students will identify the addends for a given sum.

Materials
- 2 packages of 3" x 5" (7.62 x 12.7 cm) index cards
- colored marker

To the Teacher
Having students identify the answers to addition problems is a common task. Sometimes it's done through flash cards and oral prompting ("What is 5 + 5?"). Frequently it's done with drill pages or worksheets.

A more challenging alternative, and one that allows for a variety of solutions, is to identify the addends (numbers that are added together) of a sum (the answer).

For example, the teacher may show a card that says 10. Student responses might include 9 + 1, 1 + 9, 2 + 8, 8 + 2, 3 + 7, 7 + 3, 6 + 4, 4 + 6, 5 + 5, 0 + 10 and 10 + 0!

Teacher Prep
Create a deck of sum cards. The kinds of sums you use will depend upon the ability of your students. Feel free to duplicate some of the sums, since there are several possible problems that can be matched.

The next deck of cards are the problem cards. Decide how many cards each student will be given. Five cards may be a good amount to start. Multiply that number with the total number of students playing. Write an assortment of addition problems on the cards, making sure there are one or two problem cards that reflect each sum. Shuffle the deck of sum cards and problem cards separately.

Group Activity
Introduce this game by asking students to name two numbers when added together give you __?__. Present several of these kinds of examples so students can get comfortable with the object of the game.

When you are finished, students can be dealt five cards each, faceup. Instruct them to line their cards up and examine the problems carefully. Students may want a few minutes to calculate the answers before the game starts.

Select a card from the sum deck. Cards in this deck should be drawn facedown. The teacher shows the class the card and says the number. If students have a problem card that matches the sum, students are instructed to turn the card over (from faceup to facedown). The first student who turns all five cards over correctly is the winner. Stickers can then be awarded, and the game is resumed.

 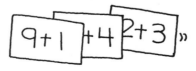

Link to Math
Try this game technique with any whole number operation: subtraction, multiplication and/or division. Older students can even "run" the game instead of the teacher!

92. Real-Life Word Problems

Math comes alive when students are the actors in problem-solving plays!

Outcome
Students will "perform" word problems in small groups. They will solve problems involving whole number operations.

Materials
- props that are used in the word problems
- video camera and tape (optional)

Teacher Prep
No preparation required other than obtaining the materials.

Group Activity
After assembling the group, select five students to perform this sample word problem:

> Mary has two blocks. Jeff has one block. Lynn has three blocks.
> Will has no blocks. How many blocks do they have all together?

Assign the roles of each character to four of the students. Distribute the suggested number of blocks to each student. The students, cued by the teacher, say how many blocks each one has. The fifth student asks the math question, "How many blocks do they have all together?" Members of the audience volunteer to answer the question.

Below are six-word problem scenarios. Divide the class into groups of four or five and assign each group a problem. Group members assemble the props necessary to perform their problem. Teacher assistance may be required in reading the word problems to the group members.

- Dana has five books. Paul and Felix each have two books. Juanita has one book. How many books do they have all together?

- Marvin has eight small cars. Brian takes two of Marvin's cars. Jake has four small cars. Suni takes one of Jake's cars. How many cars do Marvin and Jake have left?

- Audrey has seven crayons. Leo has six crayons. Marla has two crayons. Carlos has only one. How many crayons do they have all together?

- Drew has five cards. Shana has five cards. Mike has three cards. Molly takes one card from each person. How many cards did Molly take? How many cards do Drew, Shana and Mike have left?

- Dave has four paintbrushes. If he gives a brush to each of his three friends, how many brushes does he have left?

- Lucy and Julio picked six apples. They gave two of them to Henry and one to Wayne. How many apples do Lucy and Julio have left?

Link to Language
Videotape the math performances and show them during Parents' Night or Open House. If you are unable to obtain a video camera, a cassette recorder and tape will capture the audio portion of the activity. Create a stage and sets for performers and invite parents to a special performance of problem solving!

93. Roll a Problem

This dynamic dice activity will excite the math novice and expert alike!

Outcome
Students will identify the numbers on dice represented by dots and will perform simple operations using the dice.

Materials
• 1-2 pairs of dice per two students
• paper and pencil for scoring

Teacher Prep
This activity is suited for addition, subtraction and multiplication. No preparation is necessary other than obtaining the dice and pairing off students.

Group Activity
Each student rolls one die. The student who rolls the higher number goes first. Students take turns rolling the two dice and solving the problem represented by the dots. The teacher decides upon the operation: addition, subtraction or multiplication. If students are performing subtraction, remind them to subtract the smaller number from the larger one.

Every time a student gets the correct answer, he or she gets one point. If the incorrect answer is given, the student receives no points. The teacher should determine the amount of time students will be given to play. At the end of the time, students count their points to determine the winner in each pair. Stickers or similar incentives can be used as prizes.

One Step Further
Increase the complexity of the game by using more dice. For example, two red die plus two white die. Students can add the red dice (a one and a six would be 7), then the white dice (a two and a two would be 4); 7 + 4 = ? (11) or 1 + 6 + 2 + 2 = 11.

Link to Art
Obtain two large cardboard boxes that are cube-shaped. Enlist the help of students to paint the boxes with poster paints. The paint should be the same color of the dice used in class. After painting the boxes, allow them to dry. Then paint dots on each side of the cubes. Use your jumbo dice for large group math activities.

94. Addition Hopscotch

Hop to it with this fun twist on addition!

Outcome
Students will combine addition skills and large motor
activity to add a series of numbers from 1-9.

Materials

- hopscotch grid (see Teacher Prep)
- chalkboard or marker board
- chalk/pens and eraser

Teacher Prep
There are a variety of ways to make or obtain a hopscotch grid. If playing outdoors, a
grid can be drawn onto asphalt with chalk. You may want to use different colors for
each box. If playing indoors, a grid can be made on the floor using masking tape for the
boxes and numbers. A solid-colored shower curtain and masking tape will create an
indoor mat that can be easily rolled up and stored until the game is played at another
time. A final alternative is purchasing a manufactured hopscotch mat.

There can be several creative ways in organizing the hopscotch boxes and numbers.
You can vary the shapes (triangles, rectangles and squares) in which the numbers
appear; the numbers can be placed randomly in the shapes or in order from least to
greatest or greatest to least. For older students, odd numbers can be placed in squares
and even numbers in rectangles. The shapes and numbers can be color-coded as well.
It is important that whatever shapes you decide to use, they should be large enough for
every student's foot. Feel free to make the shapes slightly larger.

Group Activity
Before you start the game, practice hopping and jumping skills with your students. This
can be accomplished by playing such old-time favorites as Follow the Leader or Simon
Says.

Give students the opportunity to practice jumping from box to box on the hopscotch
grid. Depending upon ability and coordination, students can either hop to boxes with
only one foot or jump with two feet. As students play the game, the teacher should
record the numbers (on the chalkboard) as the student lands on them so everyone can
see the addends and work on the problem as the participant hops.

Game variations might include:

Color-coding boxes using yellow and orange. Students adding numbers from the yellow boxes (or orange boxes) *only* may score extra points.

Students must land on numbers from least to greatest.

Students can play Subtraction Hopscotch by subtracting the smaller number from the
larger one.

For a greater challenge, students can hop on two factors and call out the product!

Link to Science
*People are able to move
in a variety of ways: hopping and jumping to
name but two! With the
help of your students,
locate pictures of ani-
mals in magazines that
move in ways other than
walking. Frogs, rabbits
and kangaroos are
examples of animals that
hop and jump. Monkeys
not only walk and run,
but they swing! Fish
and whales swim and
so on. Create a bulletin
board display that says
"Moving Along in Room
_____."*

95. Multiplying Bunnies

Louise Mathews makes multiplication a breeze with her bunnies.

Outcome

Students will be introduced to the concept of multiplication and will use manipulatives to simulate multiplication experience.

Materials

- connecting cubes or several copies of the bunny reproducible (bottom of page)
- *Bunches and Bunches and Bunches of Bunnies* by Louise Mathews (New York: Scholastic Inc., 1978)

Teacher Prep

No preparation required other than obtaining 144 cubes or bunny cutouts.

Group Activity

This book approaches whole number operations through the "multiplying" of bunnies. The idea of this activity is to have students display the number sets as the teacher reads aloud the book. In this way, students can create number sentences that reflect addition or multiplication. Multiplication is a shorthand approach to addition. The story becomes more exciting to students as the number of sets (and numbers within the sets) grow.

One Step Further

For older, more advanced students, this book presents the concept of squared numbers: 1 x 1, 2 x 2, 3 x 3, 4 x 4, 5 x 5, 6 x 6, 7 x 7, 8 x 8, 9 x 9, 10 x 10, 11 x 11 and 12 x 12. The notation for these kinds of problems is n^2 (4^2 means 4 x 4).

Link to Science

Rabbits are fascinating mammals. There are many kinds of rabbits. They also make great pets! Have students conduct research on rabbit care using encyclopedias and pet care books.

Rabbits were an important resource to the Native Americans. Rabbit skins were often used to make warm clothing. Angora rabbits are valued today for their silky hair from which angora sweaters are made.

Enlarge and duplicate

96. Division Cups

This very important skill is approached in a very concrete way!

Outcome
Students will divide a group of objects into designated sets. They will count the number of objects in each designated set.

Materials
- connecting cubes, links, button, craft sticks or any other manipulative used for counting
- supply of paper cups
- index cards
- colored marking pen

Teacher Prep
Using the index cards, create a series of tasks such as these: 10 cubes divided among 2 cups is ____. 21 cubes divided among 3 cups is ____.

In setting up for each task, students will need to count out the number of cubes to be used with each task card, and the number of cups among which the cubes are to be divided. Demonstrate for the class how to divide the cubes. One cube is put in each cup, starting with the first cup in line. Continue placing the cubes in the cups until there are no cubes left. Count the number of cubes in each cup. This is the answer!

Group Activity
Once the activity has been modeled by the teacher, students can work either as individuals, pairs or in small groups. To make the activity self-checking, simply write the answer on the back of the task card. Students can create their own task cards to add to the teacher's collection. By establishing some simple rules, this activity can also be a game! Finally, for the purpose of whole number operations, it's important to create problems or tasks which don't involve remainders.

Link to Language
Using the numbers on the task cards, students can create their own word problems! For example: "Liza has 10 pennies. She divides them equally between her two friends, Myra and Janine. How many pennies does each friend get?"

8 cubes divided among 4 cups is ___.

2

97. Paper Plate Pizzas

Fractions find a place in children's lives when we start talking about a favorite food: pizza!

Outcome
Students will work through a recipe simulation in which the steps must follow a particular sequence.

Materials
- 9" (22.86 cm) white paper plate for each student (generic brand works best)–for the pizza dough
- red, water-base paint and paintbrush–for tomato sauce
- thinly cut pieces of yellow construction paper–for the cheese
- red or orange construction paper circles–for the pepperoni
- brown construction paper–cut and use as sausage and/or mushrooms
- plastic, resealable sandwich bags
- scissors
- glue

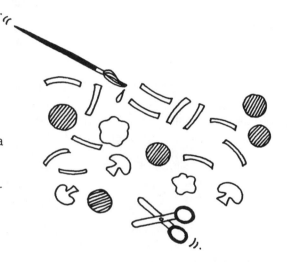

Teacher Prep
Assemble materials and arrange them on work tables. Some items may need to be precut depending upon the ability of your students. Create a sample paper plate pizza and display it at the work table.

It may also be helpful to make a fraction template from a plain paper plate. This will guide students in cutting the pizzas into *equal* pieces!

Group Activity
The project will be more manageable if the students are divided into smaller groups and assisted by the teacher. Discuss the sample with students. Students who are capable of cutting their own "toppings" should be encouraged to do so.

Emphasize the importance of following steps sequentially. For example, you would not put the tomato sauce on the dough *after* the cheese and pepperoni! When the projects are sufficiently dry, assist students in dividing the pizza into halves, thirds or fourths. If there are enough supplies, consider doing this project over several days, so each student can make a whole pizza, a pizza cut in half, a pizza cut in thirds and a pizza cut in fourths! Smaller paper plates can also be used in place of the 9" plates.

Finally, label each of the pieces 1 whole, ½, ¼ or ⅓ depending on how the pizza was divided. Store each pizza in a resealable, plastic sandwich bag.

Link to Social Studies
Plan a field trip to the local pizzeria. Watch the chef make a real pizza. Compare the number of pizza slices and their size in a small, medium and large pizza. For a culminating activity, have pizza with all of your favorite toppings for lunch.

98. Fresh Fruit Pies

This fraction activity will make your mouth water!

Outcome
Students will be introduced to the fractions ½, ⅓ and ¼ and will compare fractions to a whole.

Materials
- 4 pieces 9" x 12" (22.86 x 30.48 cm) light brown construction paper per student
- compass and protractor
- round color-coding labels: red, blue, orange, green *or* stickers: strawberry, blueberry, peach, apple
- scissors
- lamination (optional)
- resealable, plastic freezer bags

Teacher Prep
Each student will have four pies. The students can help with the decoration of the pies and the cutting (if able).

The first piece of brown construction paper should be folded exactly in half. Placing the metal point on the folded line, draw a large circle with the compass. The size of the circles must be the same for all four pies. The student then decorates the "crust" with red, round, color-coding labels, apple stickers or small paper-punched apples.

The second piece of brown construction paper should be folded exactly in fourths. Placing the metal point at the point where the two folds meet, draw another large circle. Decorate this one with blue, round, color-coding labels.

For the third piece of construction paper, draw the circle first; then using a protractor, measure every 120° to arrive at three cutting points for the pie representing thirds. After the lines have been drawn lightly for each third, students decorate this pie differently from the first two.

Finally, create a whole pie using the compass. On the back of each pie piece, write the fraction that the piece represents. When all four pies have been decorated, cut around all four circles and laminate for durability. Except for the whole, cut each of the pies into halves, thirds and fourths. Store sets of four pies in resealable, plastic freezer bags.

Group Activity
Students should start with all four pies assembled in front of them. Some questions the teacher can pose to the class are:

1. Which pie has the largest pieces?
2. How many pieces does the _____ (refer to the color or fruit) pie have?
3. Which piece is larger: one whole or one half? One half or one third? One third or one fourth? One half or one fourth?
4. Which piece is the same as 2 fourths put together?

Link to Science
Make a real pie in your classroom; no heat required! Buy a ready-made graham cracker crust in a pie tin and instant pudding (there are several flavors). Allow students to prepare the instant pudding and pour into the graham cracker crust. Chill and serve according the directions and enjoy!

99. Abacus Chips

Abacuses have been used for 5000 years, but it will only take you a minute to learn how to use it!

Outcome
Students will perform place value exercises using manipulatives.

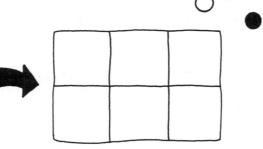

Materials
- gaming chips–three different colors (i.e. red, white, blue)
- paper

Teacher Prep
Draw a line down the middle of the paper lengthwise. Turn the paper horizontally, and draw two vertical lines separating entire paper into three columns. Duplicate one for each student. Distribute ten chips of each color to each student.

Opening Activity
The teacher should review the meaning of *ones*, *tens* and *hundreds* with students. This can be accomplished in several ways. Using overhead base ten blocks, the teacher can demonstrate or have students demonstrate how numbers are expressed with the blocks. For example, thirteen would be expressed as one rod (equivalent to 1 ten or 10) and three cubes (equivalent to 3 ones or 3). Students can be working simultaneously with base ten paper models at their desks.

Group Activity
Students start with 10 chips in each of the three lower boxes: 10 white in the lower right box (each representing 1), 10 blue in the lower middle box (each representing 10) and 10 red in the lower left box (each representing 100). The three upper boxes that are empty represent zero.

The teacher writes a number on the board, such as 37. Students, starting with the white chips (ones), move 7 to the box directly above. Then move three blue chips (tens) to the box directly above.

Adding 3 more involves moving the last three chips in the ones column, and whenever that column is empty, move all ten chips above the line down and move one chip in the tens column up.

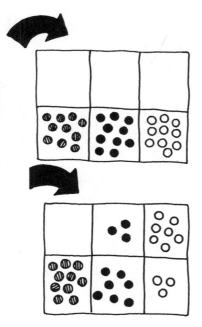

Link to Computers
Place value reduced to simple counters and columns is the basis of digital technology. Although computers perform place value functions on a binary (base two) system and our activity is base ten, it is the same concept. David Macaulay's **The Way Things Work: From Levers to Lasers, Cars to Computers – A Visual Guide to the World of Machines** *(Houghton Mifflin, 1988) dedicates a large section to how computers and the binary code works.*

100. Putting Numbers in Their Place

This hands-on activity simplifies the meaning of tens and ones.

Outcome
Students will use rods to represent tens and single units to represent ones.

Materials
- 1 blank hundreds chart per student (duplicate on card stock or construction paper for sturdiness)
- scissors
- index cards
- colored marking pen

Teacher Prep
Prepare a set of task cards by writing two-digit numbers on each card. For example: 45, 26, 11 and 72. To make the activity self-checking, draw the rod and unit answer on the back of the cards. Forty-five (four tens and five ones) is represented by four rods and five units.

Group Activity
Have students cut the one hundreds chart into nine rods and ten units. These can be stored in business-sized, letter envelopes. Students can be shown then number cards as a large or small group. Because the activity is self-checking, students can also use this as an individual or paired learning center activity.

The concept of regrouping becomes important in more advanced math. An example would be 5 tens and 13 ones = 6 tens and 3 ones. Once students have mastered tens and ones, introduce hundreds which is represented by a "square" (10 rods attached to one another). Regrouping with hundreds, tens and ones would look like this: 2 hundreds, 17 tens and 8 ones = 3 hundreds, 7 tens and 8 ones.

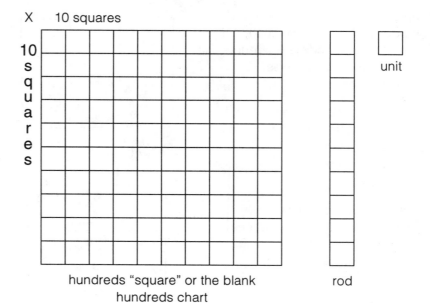

hundreds "square" or the blank hundreds chart   rod   unit

"Frog Sort," page 28
(may also be used for "A Play on Numbers," page 17)

"A Play on Numbers," page 17

M	O	N	E	Y
		FREE		

Enlarge and duplicate

Enlarge and duplicate

Math Resources

At the time of publication, every effort was made to insure the accuracy of the information included in this book. However, we cannot guarantee that the agencies and organizations mentioned will continue to operate or to maintain these current locations.

AIMS Education Foundation
P.O. Box 8120
Fresno, CA 93747-8129
(209) 255-4094

Concepts To Go®
Box 10043
Berkeley, CA 94709
(510) 848-3233

Creative Publications
5040 West 111th Street
Oak Lawn, IL 60453
(800) 624-0822

Cuisenaire Co. of America, Inc.
P.O. Box 5026
White Plains, NY 10602-5026
Customer Service (800) 237-3142

Delta Education
Hands-On Math
P.O. Box 3000
Nashua, NH 03060
(800) 442-5444

Lakeshore Learning Materials
2695 E. Dominguez Street
P.O. Box 6261
Carson, CA 90749
(800) 421-5354

The Math Learning Center
1850 Oxford Street S.E.
Salem, OR 97302
(503) 370-8130

Nasco Math
P.O. Box 3837
Modesto, CA 95352
(800) 558-9595

National Council of Teachers of Mathematics (NCTM)
1906 Association Drive
Reston, VA 22091-1593
(800) 235-7566

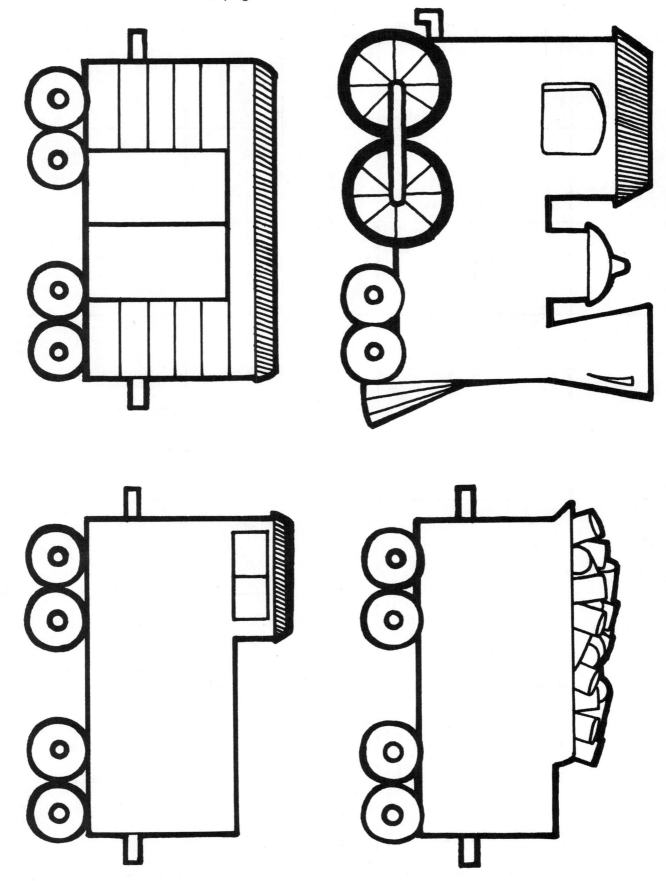